Make Thou$ands on Amazon in 10 Hours a Week

How I Turned $200 into $40,000+ Gross Sales My First Year in Part-Time Online Sales

By Cynthia G. Stine

\

For Permission Requests, please contact the publisher at:

MyPromote Books
381 Casa Linda Plaza, Ste. 288
Dallas TX 75218
214-296-0984

ISBN 10: 061557548X
ISBN 13: 978-0615575483

Acknowledgements

I am deeply grateful to my husband Tom and son Eric, who regularly put up with bags and boxes of merchandise all over the office and living room; and to Chris Green, who opens my eyes and teaches me something new every time we talk.

I'd like to thank Susan Abrahamson, Lynn Rafter, Philip Stine, Lesley Hensell and Jean Sims for giving me helpful feedback and eagle-eyed edits. Tom Nadeau of IAM Graphic Design created the cover and Elbert Balbastro helped me create a blog and Facebook fan page.

LIMITS OF LIABILITY/DISCLAIMER OF WARRANTY

This book is not affiliated with or endorsed by Amazon.com. Seller Central, Amazon Prime, 1-Click® Shopping, Amazon Web Services, Amazon.com and Fulfillment by Amazon are trademarks of Amazon.com, Inc. The happy box logo is a trademark of Amazon.com, Inc. eBay is a registered trademark of eBay, Inc. UPS is a registered trademark of UPS.

SerialMagic and SerialMagic Gears are trademarks of Serialio.com. Scanfob is a registered trademark of Serialio.com. Bluetooth is a registered trademark of Bluetooth SIG, Inc. Android is a trademark of Google, Inc. iPhone, iPad and iPod touch are registered trademarks of Apple, Inc. FBAPower, FBAScout, FBAWebScout and FBARepricer are trademarks of FBAPower.

This book covers Cynthia Stine's experiences selling online using Amazon.com™'s "Fulfillment by Amazon™" or FBA program. Results may not be typical.

Please note: Some of the products and services mentioned in this book are for products and services for which the author may earn a referral fee or commission. Even though she earns a fee on some of her recommendations, she only recommends products and services that she has used or uses herself and that she feels will deliver good value and worth. Most services have a free trial period and many offer a no-questions-asked money-back guarantee.

TABLE OF CONTENTS

People come up to Cynthia in stores, in checkout lanes and at book sales to ask what she's doing with her scanner and her piled-high baskets of goods...and she tells them. She's encouraged Big Lots cashiers to start their own online Amazon.com™ businesses leveraging their employee discount at the store; she's gotten her dad and several colleagues and friends started with their own Amazon businesses; she's pitched several "friends of the library" groups to use Amazon's Fulfilled By Amazon™ (FBA) program to raise more money for their libraries than they can from just their annual book sale; and she's shared what she's learned with seller groups on Yahoo. Her enthusiasm is infectious and she makes the business very easy to understand. She'll be the first to tell you that if she can do it, you can too.

As a 20+-year entrepreneur and marketer, Cynthia "gets" the concept of arbitrage and she knows her online customer, which makes her business efficient. Unlike eBay®, Amazon.com doesn't allow you a lot of license for clever descriptions or charming sales pitches – so how do you compete? This book will arm you with the strategies you need to make your own decisions for your business.

When I met Cynthia a year ago, her goals were modest – she wanted to pay for her son's private school while continuing with her day job. She turned a $200 investment in technology and supplies into a business that grossed more than $40,000 her first year – and that is on track to double this year. It beats the heck out of most part-time jobs and it's not pie-in-the-sky hype.

In this book, you'll learn about the tools, costs and – most importantly – strategies for making the most of your online business in the time you have available and with the financial resources you have available. She tells you exactly what she did and leads you by the hand through your first shipment to Amazon.com.

If you are interested in selling real products (books, toys, games, DVDs, CDs and more) online, I strongly suggest you read this book – and that you also use it. Plan to have your first shipment off to Amazon.com by this time next week and in a year, you'll have your own success story to share.

Chris Green

Chris Green is the owner of FBAPower™, a company that gives Amazon.com sellers the tools they need to be successful and efficient in their Fulfilled-By-Amazon business. [www.fbapower.com] His software was originally developed to help support his own thriving Amazon.com seller business. Now sellers around the country use FBAPower, FBAScout™ and FBARepricer™ for an unfair competitive advantage. In addition to developing software, he has authored "FBA Arbitrage: The Blueprint for Buying Retail Products to Sell Online for Big Profits." [http://amzn.to/chrisgreen]

Almost a year ago to the day of this writing, I was staring at my computer with dark-hollowed insomniac eyes as I tried to think my way out of my current situation. As a business owner for 16 years, I had ridden the financial roller coaster a few times, but I was out of ideas. I had moved my cheese, flipped over Fish! and tried several other smart, change-management programs.

Over the previous couple of years, I had sadly downsized my company several times until there was just me and then I moved home. My SBA loan taken out with such confidence in 2005, along with the line of credit from the bank and a credit card whose interest rate seemed to go up monthly, were costing me most of my diminished earnings every month I hadn't paid myself in some time. I realized I was literally working for my creditors every month and it was depressing. I had gone from making about $180,000 in my workaholic heyday to making zero and still working my butt off.

To add to my mood, I was worried about my family's ability to pay our bills. We love our son's private school, where all the other kids are learning-challenged as he is, but the fees and other related medical costs are more than our monthly mortgage. My husband and I agreed that if I could somehow bring in an additional $1500 a month (net) to the family, we could handle the rest with austerity measures. $1500!!! It was such a small amount and yet so far away!

I had tried so hard to bring more business into my company, but all my potential clients had hunkered down with the economy. Some of my current clients were paying late, which was part of my problem, and a few simply closed, leaving unpaid bills.

I looked around my house and thought about selling stuff, but I didn't have much to sell. I'd gone on a big selling binge in the spring through Craigslist, which was not only a big hassle, but also time-consuming. That night I decided to take a different approach. It was actually something I'd learned from Tony Robbins' 30-day program that I completed in 1990.

I keyed into my laptop the parameters of an ideal part-time business. It needed to be:

- *Reliable* – I needed money to come in regularly without having to chase the check.
- *Flexible* – I wanted to spend as much time as possible with my son after school and I still had my day job working for the creditors.
- *Simple* – my current business was complicated enough.
- *Cheap* – I didn't have any money to work with.
- *Interesting* – It had to be something about which I felt genuine *passion*. I was burned-out dealing with the creditors and payment plans. I needed to feel good again.

- *Profitable* – $1,500-$2,000 a month after expenses. I needed a big bang for my buck– minimum wage returns weren't worth my time.
- *Sustainable* – I wanted something that was recession-resistant and something I could do over and over again and get good results, unlike my current business.

For other people, this list might be different, but my priorities shifted a lot when we adopted a teenager. Once I had my criteria firmly in mind, I went looking for this ideal part-time business. In addition to running a public relations firm, I'm also an independent publisher. Books have always been a passion of mine; I probably read 250+ books a year. I come from a family with several published authors and scholars, so publishing is in my blood. I looked at my bookshelves and an idea took hold. As much as I hated to part with my paper friends, maybe there was money to be made in selling them.

I went to the Amazon.com ("Amazon") website and was absolutely overwhelmed by what I saw when I clicked the "sell your book here" link. You may have realized this too – to list a book was a real pain! It would take days and days to list my books! In addition, a lot of them were worthless – people were selling them for a penny...what in the world?! Who makes money selling books for a penny?

Then I went to eBay®; maybe it would be better there. Plus, I had some designer kids' clothes that I thought would sell. eBay was even worse! Many of the fees were upfront, I had no clue what was a good starting point for an auction, and I had to write all my own listings. This would take forever. I spent hours reading the details on eBay's site about how to sell, special selling accounts... everything. I realized this business would never work for me. It was too much to learn, it was intimidating and I don't like the uncertainty of auctions. It seemed risky to me with all the upfront and mandatory fees. Having owned my own business(es) for 17 years, I knew I'd make mistakes in the beginning and I needed to make money immediately from whatever I did.

I gave the children's clothes to a friend who is an eBay seller. We're sharing the profits after expenses and I'm thrilled–she's great at it and we both make money. In doing so, I used leverage – her time and expertise – and got rewarded for finding a super deal. This is the heart of arbitrage and the foundation for all business: Buy low, sell higher.

Next, I started looking at those "Make Money Selling Online!" books to see if someone had a better way. I found Nathan Holmquist's *Selling on Amazon's FBA Program* book and it changed everything for me. That book introduced me to Amazon's FBA (Fulfilled By Amazon) program, which was a revelation. My heart began to pound as I read the book in one sitting late at night. With FBA, I had the full might and power of Amazon behind me for a ridiculously low fee. What incredible leverage!

With FBA, you ship your books and other items for sale to an Amazon warehouse. Once the boxes get there, all your listings (conditions and pricing for your items) go live.

Amazon stores your stuff in its warehouses. They take care of the money. They ship items to your customers super-fast and then they deposit a payment directly into your bank account for your portion every two weeks – like clockwork. If there's a problem, Amazon handles all the customer relations. It was like a dream come true- my entire wish list in one program.

When I dug into the numbers, I was excited. The fees for leveraging the number-one selling platform in the world are incredibly reasonable and manageable – and you pay Amazon's commissions *after* you sell something, not before.

In this book, I am going to use my actual numbers and experience to share with you what I did, what I learned and my strategies for success. I am by no means the most successful part-time FBA seller, but I am a real seller. If I can do it, you can too. Although your goals may be different from mine, I will show you how selling on Amazon works so you can reach those goals. My hope is that you will act on this book right away and begin realizing the benefits of more income immediately.

Today I sleep better at night. I can pay my son's tuition every month and we don't have to eat beans quite so often (although I like them just fine – I am a vegetarian). I'm looking forward to doubling or nearly doubling my income in Year 2, working the same number of hours as in Year 1. I'll tell you about that, too.

You picked up this book because you need money for something very important to you – otherwise you would not be looking so hard for an answer. If my story and my explanation of the FBA program and the tools and strategies I use appeal to you – please don't hesitate. Act immediately.

You don't need to know every single detail about Amazon to be successful. I mentor several people who are learning as they go and who realized income right away. This book is a good starting point...please don't wait. You'll be glad you took action.

1

WHAT ARE YOU DOING?

I'm standing in line at Big Lots with three overflowing shopping carts of toys, books, DVDs and baby items. Someone – often the cashier – asks, "What are you doing?" They have some interesting guesses-- like I run a daycare, I'm a teacher or earth mother of the year, or I work for some children's charity. They are surprised when I tell them I'm an Amazon seller and that I do this business part-time to pay for my son's private school. Even though they work at a discount store, the idea that what they sell is actually worth a lot more surprises them.

I'll show them my tiny scanner and the software application on my cell phone that makes it easy for me to shop. I'll give them the 30,000-foot view of Amazon's FBA program and how I don't have to store tons of inventory in my house or actually ship products to my customers. I keep it simple because it is simple.

I'll tell the minimum-wage cashier with the employee discount that "You could really do well in this business just by shopping your own store." I'll hand my business card to the curious person in line behind me with many questions, and tell him to call me with questions. After a year of handing out cards, I've never gotten a call or email. It's sad, but typical.

That's how I know *you* are not typical. You are looking for extra money and you're willing to work for it. You've found this book and you're actually reading it. I commend you for this – you are already way ahead of the game. If you choose to act on what I tell you here, then you will also be way ahead of the majority of sellers on Amazon today. I don't say this because I'm a brilliant teacher with some gimmicky process, "tip" or "trick." I say this because people who sell on Amazon using its FBA program are a still a very small percentage of the sellers on Amazon. They have a tremendous built-in competitive advantage. More on that later.

Before I tell you what I'm doing, I strongly suggest you spend five minutes and jot down exactly what _you_ are doing. Why do you need the money? What will it let you do? What are your personal requirements for your business? Do you want to run it full-time or part-time? How will you measure your own success? Is it $1,000 a month? $3,000? $10,000?

Be specific and clear. For example, I am now making more than $1,500 a month with this business-- the amount I actually needed to make it worth doing. I have new goals now, like family vacations and saving for retirement, but my driving reasons are the same. If I can't make $1,500 a month on average, then it is not worth my time and I need to do something else.

"What are you doing?" Over the past year I've had friends and family ask me this question a lot. Because they know me, they know this was a serious business even though it is part-time. I'm a serial entrepreneur who has started and sold businesses. My entire 22+-year career, in one form or another, has been spent helping my clients sell products and services and build their businesses.

Some of the people I told got a gleam in their eye and jumped into the business for themselves. I suddenly found myself helping them out in a haphazard, on-demand way. I created a PowerPoint, which I walked people through. They generously gave me their feedback and asked questions...lots of questions.

That's how this book came about. I wanted to help in an organized way and I wanted a way to answer the questions that everyone asks about the business. I've structured this book around the Top Seven Questions I hear the most:

1. *Can I really make money selling stuff on Amazon?*
2. *How do you do it?*
3. *What can I sell on Amazon?*
4. *Is it hard to find inventory?*
5. *Does it take a lot of time?*
6. *What do I need to make it work?*
7. *How much does it cost to get started?*

This book is based on my experience and the experiences of my family and friends in the business who have shared some of their stories with me. It is by no means the be-all and end-all on this topic; in fact, I share the books, blogs and resources that I used and still use regularly to grow my business. I'm learning all the time from other Amazon sellers, which is part of the fun of this business.

Although others have written books containing the many tools, tips and techniques from online sellers and those who sell to online sellers, I found these books to be e very distracting and overwhelming. I looked at many different technology solutions before choosing what I use today. I spent weeks reading and researching – I wish I'd had this book to learn from myself. What I suggest for you is to follow the guidelines in this book, sell, and get some money in your pocket and experience under your belt. Then, if you want to explore all the many permutations of online selling, you will do it from a position of knowing what works. It will be much easier for you to determine how you want your business to grow and what kinds of products interest you the most.

What I hope for you is that this book allows you to make a decision – *Is selling on Amazon for me?* – and gives you the information you need to act on it right away. Every person I've told about this business who acted on it within a week has been successful – every one of them. You can be too. I may sound a little rah-rah here, but I'm not writing this book to sell it. I'm writing this book to help people change their financial situations and – by extension – their lives. If you are in a dark place as I was last year looking at bills you can't pay, I want to encourage you.

I'm an overextended mom and wife with limited resources. If I can do this, you can do this. You'll read real-world stories about a retiree looking for a certain amount of money to pay off some bills but not so much that he loses his retirement benefits; an under-employed consultant who needed to smooth the increasingly volatile income peaks and valleys with a reliable source of additional income; and a college student wanting to make some extra money for the holidays.

I'll also include some great advice given to me by my mentor in this business, Chris Green. He has been an online seller for years on eBay and Amazon and was one of the first to join Amazon's FBA program. Even though he now also sells FBA software solutions for other resellers, he is still a top Amazon FBA seller who "walks the walk" every day. He makes more in a month as an Amazon seller than many people make in a year.

I've divided this book into sections based on the Top Seven Questions listed above so it will be easy for you to go to the question that is most important to you – and to return later when you are preparing your first shipment. At the end of each section, I suggest "Take Action!" steps to help you get started.

TAKE ACTION!

1. Take a few minutes to list your personal criteria and goals for your Amazon business
2. Plan how many hours you can devote to your business this week and commit the time toward getting your first shipment out. Write it in your calendar and keep the appointment with yourself
3. Read the rest of the book

2

CAN I REALLY MAKE MONEY SELLING ON AMAZON?

Do you think selling on Amazon is only for big companies? When I first learned about FBA, I heard several horror stories from people who had tried to sell on Amazon and "didn't make any money" – depressing tales. Because people also seemed to be more familiar with the eBay model, I got questions about whether I had a big enough garage or if I was warehousing my inventory off-site. Or how I figured shipping costs...that kind of thing. Several people told me they hadn't considered selling online because they didn't have the space for storing inventory.

The beauty of Amazon's FBA program – detailed in the next chapter – is that I don't have to worry about any of those things. I let logistics superstar Amazon take care of those details. To answer the question of whether or not I actually make money selling on Amazon, I'll share with you my first-year numbers.

Year One By The Numbers

- Gross sales $41,523.42
- Net $18,242.80
  (includes holiday sales below)
- Hours per month   40
- Earned per hour $38
- Holiday sales $6,387.64[1]
  (net)
- Initial start-up costs   ~$200

It is like turning straw into gold. In the course of a year, I turned approximately $200 into $18,000+. The gross sales number represents the actual dollar amount of everything I sold.

The net figure is the amount that went into my bank account from Amazon—it's the net after paying all of Amazon's fees (commission, warehouse fee and $39.99 per month to be an Amazon Pro Seller), all my shipping costs, and the cost for FBAPower, FBAScout and FBARepricer. (I list my actual dates and deposits for you below.) What it does *not* include is the actual cost for my shipping boxes, tape, inventory, office supplies,

---

[1] From November 14, 2010 – February 6,2011.

portable scanner, inventory acquisition and some books I bought in the beginning about selling using Amazon's FBA Program. My best estimate for these costs is approximately $6,000 of which most was for inventory acquisition. Thus, my actual net was closer to $12,000 for Year 1.

Again, considering that I had about $200 to start with, I'm thrilled with these numbers. All my inventory acquisition and additional equipment was paid for out of the business as I went along. I was able to take out roughly $1,000 a month to pay for my son's private school and I'm in a terrific position for Year 2.

I didn't necessarily spend 40 hours every month on the business — that's an average. I tend to work in "bursts." As you will see, there are months in which I spent very little time on the business because I was busy with my family or my day business or whatever. Other months, I spent more time. I spent a lot of time the first three weeks in December, for example, because sales were terrific and I wanted to feed the demand. I made approximately 33% of my total year's income during the holiday season.

First Year Payouts From Amazon

Dates	Amount
9/5/2010 – 9/19/2010	-$56.10[2]
9/19/2010 – 10/3/2010	$155.69
10/3/2010 – 10/17/2010	$334.21
10/17/2010 – 10/31/2010	$450.47
10/31/2010 – 11/14/2010	$88.15
11/14/2010 – 11/28/2010	$480.02
11/28/2010 – 12/12/2010	$762.21[3]
12/12/2010 – 12/26/2010	$2,135.41
12/26/2010 – 1/9/2011	$1,244.75
1/9/2011 – 1/23/2011	$833.61
1/23/2011 – 2/6/2011	$931.64
2/6/2011 – 2/20/2011	$250.00
2/20/2011 – 3/6/2011	$498.48
3/6/2011 – 3/20/2011	$1,506.35

[2] This was my first shipment to Amazon and represented the UPS cost.
[3] I bought my first toys in early December

3/20/2011 – 4/3/2011	$1,634.93
4/3/2011 – 4/17/2011	$1,259.51
4/17/2011 – 5/1/2011	$955.45
5/1/2011 – 5/15/2011	$625.30
5/15/2011 – 5/29/2011	$251.69
5/29/2011 – 6/12/2011	$121.87
6/12/2011 – 6/26/2011	$135.21
6/26/2011 – 7/10/2011	$454.08[4]
7/10/2011 – 7/24/2011	$372.17
7/24/2011 – 8/7/2011	$376.76
8/7/2011 – 8/21/2011	$552.44
8/21/2011 – 9/4/2011	$975.97
9/4/2011 – 9/18/2011	$912.53
TOTAL:	$18,242.80

As they say in all the diet ads, your actual results may vary. I find that when I'm able to spend time, my

---

[4] We were on vacation for these two weeks and I didn't have to do a thing for my business

numbers go up. Right now, I'm sending in big shipments every week. It is "book sale season" in my area, so many of those shipments are books along with some toys. Starting in October, I'll focus heavily on toys for the holiday season.

In Year 1, I was constrained by my finances. I couldn't afford to buy any inventory in the beginning. so I used my own book and media collection as inventory. This is a terrific way to start and I recommend it for the following reasons:

- *Sunk Costs:* Your costs for this inventory were sunk long ago, so your effective cost today is $0.
- *Mistake-Friendly:* Like your first car, your first few shipments to Amazon are where you will make most of your mistakes. You might as well make them on used books and media you already own.
- *Easy Testing:* You can test pricing and ranking with very little risk to you. Want to see how long it takes to sell a book that's ranked over 1 million in terms of how fast it sells? Over 2 million? You probably have some on your shelf right now. I have a few books still in Amazon's warehouse from my first shipment last September.

- *Step-by-Step Learning:* You don't have to learn everything all at once. In other words, you can focus on "scouting" and shopping later, after you are comfortable with pricing and shipping items.
- *Pay Off Start-up Costs Faster:* The money you gain from these items can cover your start-up costs and help you acquire new inventory.

In Year 2, I expect to <u>more than double</u> what I made in Year 1 without necessarily spending any more time on the business. Why is this?

- *Latent Inventory:* I currently have <u>$37,829.50</u> in inventory (October 2011). In other words, if all those items sell for the price I want, I'll make $37,829.50 gross. That's almost as much as I made all last year. This gross sales number does not even include my last two shipments, which were quite large and represent an additional $5,000+ in latent inventory. This is a heck of a lot better than the $0 I started with a year ago.
- *Holidays:* Last year I didn't have much money to spend on toy inventory and hadn't even sold toys until December –

just books, DVDs and CDs. This year I plan to have lots of toys for sale starting in mid-to-late October. My goal is to gross $15,000-$20,000 in the holiday season alone.

- *Momentum:* This year I'm smarter, faster and better prepared. Each batch of inventory I acquire is more and more profitable and efficient in terms of money earned per hour.
- *More $ for Inventory*: I've been saving up.
- *Learning Curve:* I know so much more about the business this year that it enables me to buy more confidently and successfully. While I'm sure I will still make mistakes, I will make fewer of them.

In sharing my numbers, I hope you can see that selling on Amazon through FBA is no "get-rich-quick" scheme – and success is attainable. If you could be $12,000 richer by the end of a year, would that be meaningful to you? There are people in this business who do much, much better than I do. They have more time and they had more money for start-up costs and inventory. It really is as simple as that. If you can buy more, you can make more, faster.

My Dad wants to make $13,000 over the holidays. This is quite achievable because he has more money for inventory than I did last year.

We will talk more about how I actually did it in the next chapter.

TAKE ACTION!

- If you've not already, determine your minimum financial goals for this business. Write them down
- Determine how much you will need to make per hour (on average) to make this worthwhile for you and write this number down
- Determine how much money you have to invest in your business and write this number down. If it is only $200, then your progress will be slower but steady. If you have more for inventory, it will be faster
- Based on what you've read, is this business of interest to you so far? Why or why not? Jot down your thoughts so you can look at them when you're done with the book
- Read the rest of the book

Cynthia Stine

3

How Do You Do It?

The "beating heart" of my business is Amazon's FBA program. Here's how I do it:

- I acquire inventory at cheap prices – see "Buy Low, Sell High" later in this chapter for more.
- I use an online software program developed by FBAPower [http://bit.ly/2freeweeks] to list the condition and price of my items. This program also prints off a small label with a barcode that I put on the back of my item.
- I pack my boxes and ship them to Amazon's warehouses. I get to use Amazon's incredibly discounted shipping rate.
- At the warehouse, the items are scanned and stored for me. The minute they are scanned, my listing goes live on Amazon's site. Some of my

items have sold so quickly that they never made it off the warehouse floor into storage.

- When my item sells, Amazon handles the credit card transaction, ships the product and takes care of any customer service issues for me.

- Every two weeks (26 times a year), Amazon deposits money directly into my bank account. They take out any shipping charges, commissions and warehouse storage fees first, so the money deposited is my net.

Figure 1: My online business using Amazon's FBA Program

That's it! Of course there are details, but if you understand this, you understand why this business is so powerful for small businesses like mine...and yours.

You find good stuff to sell, and Amazon takes care of the rest.

Amazon has easy-to-understand information about how its program works. Not all of these links will work on the Kindle:

- **How it works** – http://amzn.to/FBAprogram
- **FBA guidelines** – http://amzn.to/fbaguidelines
- **How it works in the warehouse video** – http://amzn.to/warehousevideo
- **FBA fees** – http://bit.ly/FBAfees
- **Get started with Amazon FBA video** – http://amzn.to/fbagetstarted
- **Fulfillment by Amazon manual** – http://amzn.to/fbamanual

Of these videos, "get started" is best viewed after you've signed up. Otherwise it won't make much sense. It is largely aimed at current merchant sellers who want to use Amazon's FBA program.

Be sure to bookmark the Fulfillment by Amazon Manual and FBA Guidelines! They answer a lot of questions and few Amazon sellers even know these resources exist.

What You Need to Know to Get Started

For those who want to dive in and get started, go to Chapter 4. I have a checklist of the things you need to do in the first week or so to get your business in place and prepare to send your first box to Amazon. Come back to this chapter later when you want to understand how the fees and pricing work.

Fees

The biggest mistakes people make when first using the FBA program are usually around pricing and fees – and you can't price effectively if you don't understand your fees. Bear with me through this section--I'll pull it all together at the end so you can price smartly. Also, be aware that Amazon is planning to change some of its fees starting in February 2012. The fee structure will stay the same (i.e. the types of fees that Amazon charges) but some of the costs will go up. Be sure when you are creating your own pricing "rules" or guidelines that you use the most current Amazon fees.

If you don't want to read about the details behind the fees right now, jump over to page 31 where I have "the bottom line" on how the description of its fees affect my final paycheck.

Let me start by saying that Amazon makes the fees unnecessarily complicated and I can't say that I understand their logic perfectly. What I have done is set up spreadsheets and "rules" for myself so I can make good buying decisions.

Amazon charges fees for:
- Shipment to the warehouse
- Order fulfillment
- Inventory storage
- Commissions/Selling on Amazon

Shipment to the warehouse is the cost of UPS® shipping. You get the benefit of Amazon's deeply discounted rate – about 50 cents a pound – and don't even have to pay any money up front. Amazon will take the fees out of your next deposit. If you remember my deposits from last year, the first one was actually a negative number. This is because I was paying for my shipment and had not yet sold enough to cover the cost. That was my only negative payment. Amazon took it out of my bank account.

Order fulfillment covers three fees:

- Handling Fee
- Pick and Pack
- Weight per pound

The handling fee for *books* is only relevant if you use FBA to fulfill orders from other sites on which you're selling, like eBay or your own website. Because I don't sell on other sites, I've not included information in the book about this aspect of Amazon's FBA program. You can check it out here if you're interested. [http://amzn.to/multichannelFBA]. There is no handling fee for items sold on Amazon.

Pick and Pack is either 60 cents (for items under $25) or $1 (for items over $25). Lastly, there is a weight-per-pound fee of 40 cents. Weight per pound can sneak up on you when you're selling heavy textbooks.

Here's an example from Amazon of order fulfillment fees for a typical half-pound paperback:

- Weight: 0.5 lb.
- Dimensions: 8" x 6" x 2" (.056 cu. ft.)
- Selling Price: $10

Fee	Calculation	Amount
Order Handling	1 order x $0.00	$0.00
Pick & Pack	1 Unit x $0.60	$0.60
Weight Handling	.5 lb x $0.40	$0.20
Selling on Amazon Fees – varies	See Selling on Amazon Fees	
Total		$0.80 + Amazon Fee

For toys and other non-media items [media are books, videos, CDs, DVDs], the fees are different. There is a handling fee of $1, pick and pack of 75 cents (under $25) or $1 (more than $25) and weight-per-pound of 40 cents.

Here's an example from Amazon of order fulfillment fees for a digital camera:

- Weight: 2 lb.
- Dimensions: 7" x 6" x 3" (.073 cu. ft.)
- Selling Price: $70

Fee	Calculation	Amount
Order Handling	1 order x $1.00	$1.00
Pick & Pack	1 Unit x $1.00	$1.00
Weight Handling	2 lb x $0.40	$0.80
Selling on Amazon Fees – varies	See Selling on Amazon Fees	
Total		$2.80 + Amazon Fee

Inventory Storage fees kick in one month after Amazon has received your item. If your item sells in less than a month, you won't pay any warehousing fee. I currently have more than 2,400 items at the warehouse and only paid $42 in storage fees last month. This means that my storage fees are less than 1% of my total inventory per month.

The last storage unit I rented for my day job cost me $85 a month for a 10'X10' unit, which wouldn't be nearly big enough for my current inventory. And I certainly didn't have a crew fulfilling orders for me. This is a tremendous advantage of Amazon's FBA program.

Amazon has detailed measurements and weights for every item available on their site. They use these measurements and weights to assess what you owe them – it doesn't matter how many Amazon warehouses you are actually using. Right now, for example, I have items warehoused in Texas, Indiana and Pennsylvania.

Inventory fees are also seasonal. Amazon charges more for storage during the busy holiday season $.45 per cubic foot during the months of January-September and $.60 per cubic foot in October-December.

Using the paperback book in the previous example, you can see that it only costs 2.5 cents per month to store it after the first month, for most of the year. During the months of October-December, that book will cost a mere 3.4 cents to store. If that book is in inventory for 13 months (1 free month + 12 regular months), it will cost you *33 cents a year* in storage costs – a pittance.

For the digital camera, the cost is 3.3 cents per month during January-September and 4.4 cents per month October-December. For 13 months, that comes to *43 cents a year*.

At the end of my first year, I had several books in inventory from my very first shipment. These were experiments and part of my learning process. I have the choice now of leaving them there or having them removed by Amazon. Since this book is focused on getting you started, I'll cover removals – and other "maintenance" issues – in later writings.

<u>Commissions/Selling on Amazon</u> is basically your listing fee. Unlike auction sites, you don't have to pay it until the item sells. This fee is 99-cents per item. If you are selling more than 40 items a month, then you'll want to upgrade to the "Selling on Amazon Subscription Fee" of $39.99 a month, which allows you unlimited sales for this one fee. In August 2011, I sold 204 items, which means my "Selling on Amazon" fee was approximately 20 cents an item.

The other fees that are calculated under "Selling on Amazon" are commissions and variable closing fees. Amazon calls commissions "referral fees" and they vary according to category. I've printed the list here from

Amazon's site. For the most part, I'm paying 15% commissions since I primarily sell toys, games, baby products, office products and media items.

Referral Fees

Product Type	Referral Fee Percentage
Amazon Kindle	15%
Automotive Parts and Accessories	12%
Baby Products (excluding baby apparel)	15%
Beauty	15%
Books	15%
Camera and Photo	8%
Cell Phone Accessories	15%
Clothing & Accessories	15%
Consumer Electronics	8%
Grocery & Gourmet Food	15%
Health and Personal Care	15%
Home & Garden (including Pet Supplies)	15%
Industrial & Scientific Supplies	12%
Jewelry	20%
Kindle Accessories	25%
Music	15%

Musical Instruments	12%
Office Products	15%
Personal Computers	6%
Software & Computer Games	15%
Sporting Goods	15%
Tires & Wheels	10%
Tools & Home Improvement	12%
Toys	15%
Video & DVD	15%
Video Games	15%
Video Game Consoles	8%
Watches	15%
Unlocked Cell Phones	8%
Any Other Products	15%

Variable Closing Fee Schedule

Media Product Type	Variable Closing Fee
Books	$1.35
Music	$0.80
Videos (VHS)	$0.80
DVDs	$0.80
Video Games	$1.35
Video Game Consoles	$1.35
Software & Computer	$1.35

Games	

Variable Closing Fees are assessed for processing the order through Amazon. Think of it as the fee Amazon charges you for using its credit card processing system and for any customer support that might be needed for that item.

For media, they charge a flat fee (see above) per item. There is no variable closing fee on the sale of non-media products fulfilled using the Fulfillment by Amazon™ service. So while you'll pay a $1.35 variable closing fee for selling a computer game, you won't pay a variable closing fee on a Barbie doll. To be clear, what you *will* pay instead on the Barbie doll is the commission fee. For a $45 Barbie, that works out to $6.75. I know this is confusing. The most important thing to remember from this discussion of fees is that they exist. Even if you don't understand them, if you can allow for them in your pricing, you'll do fine. Amazon lists all fees on its site as well.

FEES: BRINGING IT ALL TOGETHER – HOW DO YOU KNOW YOU ARE MAKING A PROFIT?

Standing in front of a shelf of Barbie dolls or discounted best-seller books is not the time to calculate fees and profits. Early on, I devised some "rules" for myself that allow me to shop with confidence. I calculated fees and profits for a typical item in each category in which I sell, and then used it as my starting point. I know for how much I *must* sell an item to make it worthwhile.

The chart shows actual numbers from products I sold last month. I estimated a per-unit cost ("miscellaneous expenses") for boxes, tape, UPS pick-up fees, barcode labels, software subscriptions, etc. – the cost of doing business – based on the number of units I shipped to Amazon last month.

I did not include taxes because I now buy most of my items sales-tax-free. Of course I do pay taxes later, but the numbers are unpredictable as they are based on the actual price for which the item is sold. As I go to press, Amazon is introducing a program in 2012 where it will collect sales taxes for the State of Texas (where my business is based) for me.

In the spreadsheet on the next page, you'll notice that I include the actual dollars that Amazon sent me *and* I show my net after my other expenses. In the paperback example, I turned 10 cents into 60 cents.

Of course, it is more fun and efficient to make $33.78 from a 25-cent investment like the Jane Fonda workout video (see chart).

Lastly, I show you my personal minimum prices. When I'm at a book sale looking at paperbacks, for example, I take my minimum price; add the actual cost of a paperback at the sale (say 50 cents) and that is the smallest amount I must see on my scanner in order to buy the book. (The scanner shows the current offers for that product online).

If you look at *Red Dragon*, you see that my out-of-pocket expenses on this paperback are $2.71 not including the cost of the book. If I sell that book for $4 (assuming no cost for the book – if I already owned the book, let's say), then I'll make a 60-cent profit. Because I buy most of my books today, I need to add the acquisition cost to the $4.00. If the book at the book sale is 50 cents, then I need to see a minimum of $4.50 selling price on my scanner to make it worthwhile to buy the book. In that case, I would make a profit of 60 cents

Many of the books I buy at book sales are selling online for $6 to $9, which gives me a nice margin.

	Red Dragon	Grandfather's Son memoir	Biology
	Paperback Book	Hardback Book	Textbook
Actual sales price	$4.00	$6.25	$35.00
Amazon Fees			
- Commission	($0.60)	($0.94)	($5.25)
- FBA per-unit fee	($0.60)	($0.60)	($1.00)
- FBA weight-based fee	($0.22)	($0.52)	($2.06)
- Variable closing fee	($1.35)	($1.35)	($1.35)
Shipping	$1.49		
Promo Rebate	($1.49)		
TOTAL DEPOSIT FROM AMAZON:	**$1.23**	**$2.84**	**$25.34**
Acquisition cost	($0.10)	($1.00)	($2.00)
Other costs			
- Subscription fee $39.99/month	($0.20)	($0.20)	($0.20)

	Red Dragon	Grandfather's Son memoir	Biology
- Shipping estimate (to warehouse)	($0.25)	($0.50)	($2.50)
- 1 month storage fee	($0.025)	($0.035)	($0.06)
- Miscellaneous expenses	($0.06)	($0.06)	($0.06)
TOTAL OTHER EXPENSES	($0.635)	($1.80)	($4.82)
NET PROFIT (rounded):	$0.60	$1.05	$20.52
MINIMUM OUT-OF-POCKET EXPENSES (not incl. acquisition cost or commission fee):	$2.70	$3.26	$7.23
MY PRICING MINIMUMS FOR THE CATEGORY:	$4.00	$5.00	$10.00

[Don't forget to add your actual acquisition cost to the pricing minimum when scouting.]

	Jane Fonda	Melrose Place	Cranium Jr.	Bob-the-Builder Potty Seat
	VHS	Software/ DVD/CD	Toy	Baby
Actual sales price	$42.95	$26.98	$25.00	$24.95
Amazon Fees				
- Commission	($6.44)	($4.05)	($3.75)	($3.74)
- FBA per-unit fee	($1.00)	($1.00)	($1.00)	($1.00)
- FBA weight-based fee	($0.15)	($0.32)	($1.00)	($0.75)
- Variable closing fee	($0.80)	($0.80)	($1.26)	($0.22)
Shipping		$5.32		
Promo Rebate		($5.32)		
TOTAL:	$34.56	$20.81	$17.99	$19.24
Out-of-pocket cost	($0.25)	($5.00)	($6.00)	($8.00)
Other costs				
- Subscription fee $39.99/month	($0.20)	($0.20)	($0.20)	($0.20)
- Shipping estimate (to warehouse)	($0.25)	($0.25)	($1.00)	($0.25)
- 1 month storage fee	($0.020)	($0.030)	($0.050)	($0.025)
- Miscellaneous expenses	($0.06)	($0.06)	($0.06)	($0.06)
NET PROFIT:	$33.78	$15.27	$10.68	$10.71

	Jane Fonda	Melrose Place	Cranium Jr.	Bob-the-Builder Potty Seat
MINIMUM OUT-OF-POCKET EXPENSES (not incl. acquisition cost or commission fee):	$2.48	$2.66	$4.57	$2.51
MY PRICING MINIMUMS FOR THE CATEGORY:	$3.00	$3.50	$6.00	$5.00
[Don't Forget to add your actual acquisition costs to these numbers when scouting]				

If you look at the Bob-the-Builder Potty Seat pricing minimum, you will see that I need to add the $8 acquisition cost to the $5 pricing minimum and see $13 on my scanner to make it worth buying. In actuality, I like better margins than that on toys and baby items due to their extreme price fluctuations and the fact that Amazon tends to be aggressive in its own pricing in these categories. Also, I'm paying more out of pocket so I want a higher return for my inventory investment. For non-media categories, I want to see 3X or better on my scanner, or three times the acquisition cost. That's what makes the potty seats so terrific – they sell for nearly $25 online and I'm only paying $8. They also sell like crazy. I wish I had hundreds of them. I cover "scouting" and pricing in more detail later in the book.

PAYMENTS

This is the most exciting section of the book: payment! When you set up your account on Amazon, you have the option of direct deposit every two weeks. Here are just a few things to know:

- **Tax ID number:** If you don't have a business set up yet or a business banking account, set that up first. It will make accounting easier for you later.

- **Escrow:** You won't get paid everything you are owed in the beginning. The first two weeks Amazon builds up an escrow account of your money and holds on to it. This escrow is to cover future shipping charges, refunds and other activities for which they may need to charge you down the road. Once you prove yourself and build up funds in your account, they'll release the money.

- **Four-day lag:** It takes four days for the payment to get into your bank account from Amazon. If they distribute on a Sunday, you get paid on a Thursday.

- **Taxes:** You are expected to pay your own taxes *although* this is changing. They have just introduced an option where they will collect your taxes from your customers for you for a small fee. To my mind, this is a no-brainer and I've signed up — calculating my state taxes is one less thing I have to worry about. I believe this new program goes into effect in January 2012.

- **Reports:** Amazon keeps real-time reports online of all your sales transactions, their fees and your net profits. They also send you an email when a payment is sent to your bank account.

REPORTS

Amazon provides a dizzying list of reports for you to manage your business. You can access them through your Amazon Seller account once it is set up. These include:

- **Inventory** – everything relating to your inventory. From the inventory page, you can go to your shipping queue, download inventory reports, change prices, delete items from inventory and more.
- **Payments** – shows sales you have made for any given period, who bought your

items and from what state. This is where you will keep track of your pending (and past) payments from Amazon. In addition, you can look at individual transactions to see Amazon's fees and your net profit.

- **Amazon Selling Coach** – covers ways you can improve your sales and statistics on your inventory.
- **Business** – gets into the nitty-gritty of your sales by date, by SKU (your personal identifier for each product), by site views and more. I rarely use these, given the short amount of time I have to focus on this business every week.

KNOW YOUR CUSTOMER

FBA sellers have access to different customers than other Amazon sellers, also known as "merchant sellers." In particular, your target customer is the Amazon Prime Member. Amazon Prime is a program that gives members free two-day or greatly reduced one-day shipping on all orders, free video downloads and more. Prime members even have a different view of the site when they visit. If you are not a Prime member now, you may want to join at some point as a way to understand your customer. The cost is $79 a year.

Prime members can – and often do – search solely by Prime-eligible offers – a huge competitive advantage for FBA Sellers because these Prime members don't even see offers from competitive merchant sellers

Here are the characteristics of Amazon Prime members:

- Impatient
- Internet savvy
- Frequent online shoppers
- Loyal – will often use the site without checking other sites
- Fans of Amazon's shipping and customer service

- Price-resistant – buyers who will pay a premium for better and faster service
- Will pay more for the peace of mind of working with Amazon
- Will buy from multiple categories, not just media

In short, Prime members are Amazon's biggest spenders and most frequent users. Amazon estimates that Prime members spend on average $500 *more* per year than typical site visitors. They are the most valuable customers on Amazon's site and now they are your customers. When you list your item as Fulfilled By Amazon, Prime members know that their product will be shipped directly from the warehouse to them by Amazon, rather than from a merchant (third-party) seller. The item will also be covered by Amazon's famous "A-to-Z" satisfaction guarantee and world-class customer service, neither of which is the case when buying from merchant sellers.

This advantage is so powerful that even non-Prime members will be drawn to the FBA seller. Last month, 44% of my sales were to Prime buyers, which is not surprising. What is astounding is that 56% of my customers were not Prime buyers! Why is this so amazing? I usually charge more than the merchant sellers, and I rarely have the lowest-priced offer. *My customers are so loyal to Amazon and pleased with its service that they will pay a premium for it.*

Another reason that so many non-Prime members may have been attracted to my merchandise is the Amazon "buy box." As an FBA seller, I am eligible for and frequently listed in the buy box, which means that mine is the first offer a visitor sees. They can click on my name, have the item paid for through Amazon's "one-click" payment system and be done with the order in less than a minute.

Amazon only sells new merchandise, which immediately puts your used books and media at an advantage. Now the Prime buyer can get used media expedited the same way as with new.

As I mentioned earlier, when a Prime member logs in, their site is a little bit different. Offers eligible for free shipping are highlighted in their searches ahead of merchant-fulfilled items. Think about that. Even if a merchant seller is offering a lower price than you, *your item will come up first* because you are the FBA seller. This is a huge competitive advantage! Certainly with a few more clicks a Prime buyer can look at all the offers if desired, but most of them do not – they prefer to buy Prime for the reasons previously cited

We'll talk more about this later under pricing strategies.

Customers who are either Amazon Prime members or whose total order will be over $25 qualify for free shipping. Clicking this button helps them find the offers they want.

In this case, I am the only FBA seller.

LEVERAGE TECHNOLOGY

The beauty of this business is that it is technology-enabled. You don't need a warehouse or a lot of new equipment to get going. If you already have a home office and/or a computer, you have most of what you need to get started. In this section, I'll identify the tools I use. Later in the book, I will walk you through step-by-step until your first shipment is on its way to Amazon.

Inventory Tracking and Posting Software – I use FBAPower [http://bit.ly/2freeweeks], an online subscription program that makes it easy for me to prepare my listings for Amazon, print off barcode labels for my items and ship to the correct warehouse. I create unique SKUs (stock-keeping units) that help me keep track of my items, including where and when I bought them. The first two weeks are a free trial. If you click on [http://bit.ly/2freeweeks], you'll get an extra two free weeks – an entire month total – to try it. FBAPower is the first service I used, for listing my personal library of books.

These two videos give you an idea of how it works: http://bit.ly/fbapower3 http://bit.ly/fbaspeedtest

USB Scanner – You will need some kind of handheld scanner to read the ISBN#s and UPC codes on the back of your books and other inventory. Buy a cheap one for $25 to sit by your computer. If you are low on start-up funds, just get FBAPower and a scanner to process your home library of books, DVDs, CDs, VHS tapes, software, audio books, etc. Sell stuff from your family and neighbors (share profits with them). As your items sell, you'll be able to afford more tools and inventory.

Label Printer – FBAPower generates small labels with your unique barcode that you will put on the back of your merchandise (covering the ISBN#). If you have a label printer at your desk, you can quickly print the label, put it on the product and drop it in a box. If you are short on funds, you can wait to buy a label printer because Amazon will create labels for you that print on 8.5"x11" sheets of stickers. This service is free but it is also more time-consuming because you have to match labels to items, which can be a pain if you have more than 10-20 unique items. When you are ready to buy a label printer, get either a LabelWriter or a Zebra. I have the LabelWriter 450 Turbo, which costs about $70 on Amazon. I've also seen them for sale (used of course) more cheaply on Craigslist.

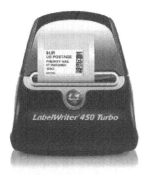

Portable Database – When scouting for new inventory, you need the freshest possible information to make a good decision. I originally started with ASellerTool's solution. It worked fine for books. It was cumbersome, though, because I had to download the Amazon database to a personal digital assistant (PDA), which often took hours — and even then it couldn't hold the entire database, so sometimes items were missing. The data would also get old fast so I'd have to re-load the database every single night. And it did not show FBA offers, either. There was a lot of guessing and luck with ASellerTool, but it was among the better tools available at the time.

In November 2010, FBAPower launched FBAScout, which knocks the stuffing out of any other scanner out there. It consists of two parts: an application that runs on smartphones (phones with Android™ operating system and iPhone® phones), iPod touch® or iPad®; and a tiny Bluetooth™ laser-scanner that reads barcodes and transmits the numbers into FBAScout on your phone.

FBAScout is unique because it shows you FBA offers. In addition, it connects real-time to Amazon so the data is current as of that minute. This video has more information: http://bit.ly/fbascoutbenefits.

Image reprinted with permission from
FBAPower. ©2010

As you can see, the data is neatly organized for quick decisions. At a glance I know that I want this book (assuming I'm paying $3 or less for it) because its ranking is very low (253) and the lowest FBA seller price is $10.73. The letters after the price tell me the condition. "VG"= "very good," "N"= "new," and so on. I compare the condition of the book I want to buy against the condition of the other (same) books offered for sale.

The weight of the book also figures into my consideration (remember my chart with the paperback, hardback and textbook) as does the Amazon department in which it will be listed. Be sure to look at the department pulled up by FBAScout before deciding to buy. The listing department for books is obvious, but the listing department for some items, like calendars, isn't clear and you have to look at the category carefully.

For example, you can find calendars in both the Books and Office Supplies departments, and the rankings in each department are very different. Software, video games and DVDs can sometimes be found in books, sometimes in toys, sometimes in video games. If you don't know the appropriate category, you can make a mistake and buy something that will take months or years to sell. FBAScout gives you the information you need to make shopping almost foolproof.

Another advantage of FBAScout – one that has opened up my business tremendously – is the fact that it will give you prices for virtually any item with a barcode. Now, in addition to books, I also sell toys, games, home goods, pet supplies, baby items and more with complete confidence. I find the financial returns are often better with these items than with books. All the other scout tools on the marketplace are targeted toward books and media only. With FBAScout I am limited only by my curiosity.

The day I got my Scanfob® and FBAScout (December 3, 2010) is the day I officially became an

Amazon seller rather than an online bookseller. Because the fob is tiny, I wear it around my neck with a lanyard so I don't have to worry about dropping it or losing it.

I also use a wristband to carry my smartphone so I can use both my hands as I shop. I scan, look at the smartphone on my wrist, decide and go to the next item.

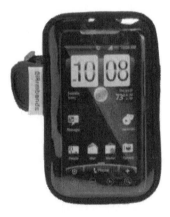

When I shop, I wear a fanny pack so I'm completely hands-free. In my pack, I carry tissues (you wouldn't believe how dusty a book sale can be), a permanent marker with a fine tip, my checkbook/credit cards and a backup battery for my phone and Scanfob. The battery is essential for marathon shopping days – I can plug in my depleted phone or Scanfob and keep shopping. I have never used up the battery pictured next – it's a humdinger.

Another item you will need at some point is a dolly for carrying book boxes – I have several. One is a large, industrial dolly that I bought at Sam's Club for about $80. It can be pulled as a flatbed cart or used in the upright position. It carries up to 900 pounds and helps me move heavy boxes around my house (I've stacked nine on it before) and out to the car or front porch. I also have a smaller fold-up dolly that is great for carting two or three boxes around a book sale. It is small, maneuverable and beats the heck out of carrying a heavy bag. I got my small dolly for $25 at Sam's Club and have since seen a similar one for $20 at Big Lots.

Harper Industrial Dolly. Converts to flat-bed.

The Amazing Pocket Chair® is a new addition to my gear for book sales. I nearly ruined my knees at one book sale, digging around in the boxes underneath the tables. Never again! This chair is small, portable and just the right height for scanning through boxes on the floor. It comes in a small bag with a handle that I can hang on my dolly. I got mine for $6 at Big Lots; they're also sold on Amazon: http://amzn.to/amazingpocket.

Repricing Software – Although I don't talk about it much in this book, a repricing solution is critical once your inventory gets too large to handle manually. I tried several options over the past year and didn't like them because I could not get them to price exactly to my criteria. FBAPower just came out with its FBARepricer and I like it much better. It takes into account the other FBA offers and is tailored to FBA sellers, whereas other programs are focused on merchant sellers. FBARepricer comes free with FBAPower for up to ten repricings a month; if you want more repricings than that, there is a modest fee structure.

FBAPower and FBAScout can be bought separately for $39.95 each or subscribed to as a bundle for $59.95 (with FBARepricer).

MORE ON PRICING: BUY LOW, SELL HIGH

In the earlier discussion of fees, I shared with you my minimum starting point for pricing, for several types of items. Before you branch into a different category, I encourage you to run some numbers yourself so you'll be sure to know the "floor" for your prices. Your expenses may be different from mine, which may affect your floor. Amazon is changing its fees, so you also need to make sure you adjust for this.

Some categories, like toys, are also difficult to price because the product sizes, weights, shipping costs and prices vary so wildly. In addition, you never know when Amazon or another FBA seller will start a price war and slash prices. That's why I have a "rule of thumb" for pricing new merchandise that Chris Green taught me – 3X. Whatever the cost of the toy/appliance/electronic item, if I'm able to sell it for at least three times the cost, I'll probably be OK.

Last Christmas, several of us were selling "Dippin' Dots" toys for $65 and up. After Christmas, the price quickly dropped to around $30. Because I had bought mine for around $24, I wasn't worried about clearing out my final units – and they're selling again, for $78 this time around.

In the potty seat example earlier, I bought the seat for $8 and sold it for $24.95, making $10.71 in net profit – Wow! Wow because who would pay $24.95 for a plastic toilet seat? And wow because I turned an $8 investment into 133% return in two weeks. (Those seats sell like crazy.) I'd like to see the stock market achieve that kind of return on investment.

This brings me to the next very important consideration when deciding what to buy – speed of the sale, otherwise known as "ranking."

Buy High-Turnover Items

Even though Amazon's warehousing fees are cheap, you don't want your inventory to sit around – you only make money when something sells. So how do you know how fast something will sell? Rank.

Amazon has millions of items in its warehouses at any given time. The faster and more recently an item has sold, the lower it will be on the rank scale. Amazon calls it *velocity*. Number one on the rank scale is selling the most units per minute; number 10,000,000 may not have sold a single item in years. *However,* it is important to note that ranking is only a snapshot in time and not indicative of future sales. If a book ranked 10,000,000 were to sell today, its ranking might drop down to 80,000 tomorrow because a sale was made the day before. I have author friends who find this very puzzling. One minute the book they wrote is ranked in the millions, and the next day it is ranked around 80,000 or less. All that indicates is that sales were made recently, which dropped the ranking. If no further sales are made, the ranking will quickly climb back up. Amazon does not share its secret formulas, algorithms or sales data, so you have to make a best guess. I use rank to indicate that an item will sell. I've sold books with ranks over 2 million, but they took a long time to sell. Generally, I won't buy a book or media item that is ranked over 1 million unless the potential payoff is worth the potential warehouse fees. Because I had so little money to invest in inventory last year, I could not wait for a big payoff.

As of September 26, 2011, this was the number-one-selling book on Amazon, selling thousands a day. The "Top 100" list is updated hourly.

The number-one-ranking toy (*and* baby toy) on Amazon on September 26, 2011. It sells for around $6.

The number-one video game on Amazon on September 26, 2011.

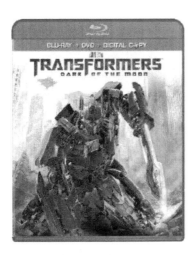

The number-one DVD on Amazon on September 26, 2011.

Another thing Chris taught me about this business is that I have no idea what is popular. That's why it is so crucial to scan everything and not guess. Would you have guessed that a plastic ball would be the number-one-selling item on Amazon in toys? Now, the popularity of *The Son of Neptune* doesn't surprise me — it's already on my Kindle.

Earlier, we talked about fees and pricing, which are important for decision-making. Now we add in rank. If an item is ranked high, it will probably take a long time to sell; At minimum, you know it has been a while since one was sold. Although Amazon's storage fees are amazingly cheap, I'm not making any money if I'm not selling. So what is a good rank on Amazon?

I'm sorry to say, Amazon won't tell you. All Amazon has said in the past is that in books, items that are 100,000 and under will generally sell within a month (and often many copies within a month), and items that are between 100,000 and 1,000,000 will often sell within three months. I try to buy items ranked under 1,000,000 for this reason. Sometimes I will make exceptions if the return on investment is worth it. For example, I had two phonics reading programs that I bought new at Big Lots for $20 each and sold for $165 each. The first one took about six weeks to sell; the second one took an additional three months. It was worth the wait to me; in fact, I wish I could find more. I was also the only FBA seller.

I've listed my buying criteria in the chart below. Let me stress here that it is _my_ criteria and I do not have all the answers. As you get into the business, you will conduct your own experiments and find the range with which you are most comfortable. Other FBA sellers may also tell you their criteria. In the beginning, when you are focused on fast cash, stay toward the low-ranked items and don't invest in long-term payoffs – no matter how tempting – until you can afford it. My "exceptions" column is where I personally might buy if the payoff was exceptional – $30 for a 25-cent book, for example. This has changed over time for me as I made more money and could afford to wait a little bit. You'll have your own "exceptions" column. I'm still learning about selling CDs, software and video games and cannot tell you what the "best" range is – only where I know I've made sales.

	Ideal rank	Upper limit	Exceptions
Books, Audio Books, Calendars	1-100,000	1,000,000	2,000,000
Textbooks	1-500,000	1,500,000	2,000,000
VHS	1-1,000	5,000	250,000
DVDs	1-100,000	500,000	
CDs	1-100,000	don't know	
Software	1-1,000	16,000 so far	
Video games	1-200	don't know	
Toys	1-75,000	165,000	
Baby	1-30,000	don't know	
Pets		don't know	
Home Improvement	1-20,000	don't know	
Electronics	Amazon does not provide rankings for many electronics; I don't know why.		

One caveat with textbooks is that they are seasonal. They generally sell briskly in late August/September, January and June. If you are scanning in March and the textbook is ranked1,000,000, it is worth a look – especially if the condition is very good – because its rank will go down during the peak selling seasons. Obviously the lower the rank the better, but I've sold textbooks for over $100 that were above 1,000,000 in rank. The higher the rank, the higher the reward I want to see.

VHS videotapes are niche products, so I don't buy them if the ranking is above 5,000 unless the video is very specialized and not available in other formats. For example, I bought a rare 1991 video of *Cyrano de Bergerac* for 25 cents and sold it for $25. Its ranking was 218,714. I sent it to Amazon in mid-October 2010 and it sold on May 9, 2011 – about six months. Not bad for a 25-cent investment.

With DVDs, I've not found the upper limit yet. So far, I find plenty of merchandise within these ranges and there's been nothing of such great value at a high rank that I'll risk it sitting at the warehouse for months to a year.

I've not sold a lot of software above 15,000 in rank. Often software that I buy is listed for sale in "toys" rather than "software," because it is a learning game for youngsters. I sold a "Top Chef" game that ranked around 16,000 in software. I sent it in March and it sold at the end of August – just over five months.

Like calendars, DVDs/games/videos don't always appear where you might think on Amazon.com. Once a product is listed on Amazon, you are generally stuck with that category. The category is usually chosen by the person who listed the item. For this reason, it is important to look at the category when you are scanning. You will NOT be able to list the product in a different category and 100,000 in toys is different than 100,000 in software.

I've recently found a source of cheap used video games (10 cents) and I'm experimenting with them right now.

Toys sell year round, but go crazy during the holidays. Even higher-ranked items (around 100,000) will sell quickly during this time and, in addition, selling prices are often higher. I've sold many Wii Sureshot Rifles since December 2010, starting at $30. They still rank in the low hundreds. I sold one in October 2011 at $19.50, just to give you an idea. As long as I can get them cheaply enough, I don't mind – but I'm really looking forward to the holidays again.

For baby items, I'm still experimenting to get an upper range. Generally, I buy things under 30,000 in rank. I avoid items that might be subject to a recall like car seats, strollers, cribs, etc. This is just my philosophy – I don't want the hassle should that happen. I've sold everything from baby wipes to bottles, pacifiers and spoons, to diaper bags, potty seats and booster seats. And, of course, lots of baby toys. Sometimes they are listed for sale in Amazon's baby department, and sometimes in toys – be sure to check before buying.

Ironically, everything I've ever bought in "pets" ended up appearing in the "kitchen and dining" category. I've sold pet toys in this category that have ranked around 100,000; they took around three months to sell.

Some wall stickers I bought sold in "home improvement." I sent them to Amazon in June; the slowest-selling one ranked just over 5,000 and took two months to sell, while the others—one ranked over 19,000—sold in June and July. That just goes to show that you can't predict customer behavior precisely with rank.

The best sources of ranking advice are other FBA sellers. One of the resources listed in the back of this book is the FBA Forum Yahoo! group [http://bit.ly/fbayahoogroup], a group committed to helping other FBA sellers be successful. I've learned a lot from them.

GO WHERE OTHERS ARE NOT

When I walk into a store like Big Lots, I know I am the only scout there and I focus on low-hanging fruit and the categories that usually give me the highest rewards. When I go to the "members-only" night of a big book sale, I look around and go to where the other scanners are not. The fiction tables are usually crowded, while the textbook and non-fiction tables are not. At one sale, I went to the VHS tapes first and got some great bargains. (See my earlier Jane Fonda example.) VHS tapes are nearly always 25 cents at book sales and thrift stores, or even 10 for a $1, so there is good potential there. I want to avoid fighting for inventory *and* I want to find inventory where there are not a lot of other FBA sellers.

My best returns on investment are where I am the only FBA seller or I am one of maybe two or three, tops. For the past six months or so, I've sold a foam booster seat on Amazon for $45 where I was not only the sole FBA seller, I was the only seller, period. I sold at least one a day when I had inventory. As of last week, I've been discovered – there are now four FBA sellers with my booster seats. I'm still selling mine for around $45, but I know the prices will start to drop as the others compete, so I'm looking for my next great deal.

To do this, I need to shop where the others are not. While I love Big Lots – and have many categories for which I still need to scan – I know many other FBA sellers buy there too. Thus, I've branched out. I try to keep my scanner with me at all times.

One day at the Blockbuster video store. I saw a couple of tables of items that were completely unrelated to videos, like an "as seen on TV!" vacuum cleaner, some toys, books, wall stickers...it was a wild mix. Everything was at least 75% off and some items were $1. I ended up buying most of the inventory and then going to other Blockbuster Video stores in my area for more. I sold the $1 wall stickers for $15, the $3 stuffed Star Wars toys for $21, the $10 vacuums for $40 and much, much more. I was usually the only FBA seller for these items and most of my inventory sold out in less than two weeks, with the rest selling over the next two months. The wall stickers were an experiment – I had never sold in the home décor category and had no idea what was a good ranking.

TEST, TEST, TEST

Chris Anderson wrote a book called *The Long Tail,* which explains that there is a buyer for almost everything and that platforms like Amazon offer an efficient way for people to reach their audiences, no matter how small. The "niche culture," as he calls it, is a growing worldwide phenomenon. This is why I picked up *Cyrano de Bergerac* and other unusual items even though I knew they were not fast sellers. You will run across items like this as well and may decide to take a chance.

My friend Lesley has had success with some very old books that didn't even have ISBN#s (pre-1972), but that sold well once she was able to find Amazon's ID number. One exciting find cost her a dollar and is so valuable that she's going to broker the sale through a rare book dealer. Although you won't find a book worth $1,500 at most book sales, you can.

I am constantly testing. Nearly every shopping trip will include some kind of experiment, whether it is the Milk-Bone brand dog toys, the adult diapers, the closet organization tool...you get the idea. The only way I'm going to learn about different categories is by testing. I don't have a lot of money, so I start small. With toys, I was lucky because Chris Green took me on a shopping trip with him to Big Lots and I learned a lot. I was able to participate in the holiday season with confidence.

As a side note, shared information is more valuable than stolen information. Some FBA sellers try to take shortcuts to learning by browsing the Amazon pages of other FBA sellers and copying their purchases. Although I find this practice annoying, I know I'm in a better position than they are because I know *why* I listed a certain item and they don't. They are just hoping I'm smart and thus worth copying.

My goal with this book is to make _you_ smart so you know what a good deal looks like and can make decisions that are profitable for you.

BE A JOINER

Big Lots, Toys "R" Us, Home Depot, Sears, Kmart, jcpenney and many other retailers have customer loyalty programs that you'll want to join. They are free and give you several advantages:

* Advance notice of sales
* Special discounts and offers
* The ability to earn even greater rewards
* Online-only offers

Big Lots, for example, has a special toy sale in December with huge discounts for "Buzz Club" reward members; members get to shop the deals several days before the public does. In addition to the discounts, Big Lots gives its loyalty members coupons good for 20% off everything after 10 qualifying sales. Chris and I attacked last year's sale, and had about six baskets of toys between us. My only regret was that I had such a limited inventory budget and therefore couldn't buy as much as I wanted to.

Toys "R" Us, Wal-Mart and Target have sales, coupons and online-only deals. You can also order in quantity online if you find something hot. Sometimes they offer free shipping for orders over a certain amount, or on certain days (like Cyber Monday).

I've not yet joined Home Depot or Lowes loyalty programs simply because I have all I can handle right now without getting into another category. A colleague of mine sells tools, which is how I learned about their programs.

Sam's Club and Costco charge an annual membership fee, but there are good deals to be found there – particularly if you can afford to buy in quantity. Chris Green told me about a product that he bought at Sam's a year or two ago for nearly $1,000 that he was able to turn in about a week for $2,000. He became the Club's number one buyer of that product and they ordered just for him. I don't have that kind of financial muscle right now where I can invest thousands in inventory every month – but someday I will.

TAKE ACTION!

* Review Amazon's FBA program and Prime Membership on the website until you understand how both work
* Become an Amazon Prime member if you are not already (or plan to become one when you can afford the annual fee)
* Determine your inventory on hand to get started. Do you have books? CDs? DVDs? VHS tapes?
* Are you already a member of Sam's Club or Costco? Get on their mail and email lists
* Join email lists for Toys "R" Us, Big Lots, jcpenney, Kmart, Sears, Home Depot, Lowes and others so you can get their online sales flyers

4

CHECKLIST OF WHAT TO DO *NOW?*

This chapter is for my friend Lynn who said, "Just tell me what I need to do right now – 1, 2, 3, 4." This plan of action assumes that you will start with new and used items around your house. According to studies, the average household has over $5,000 of sellable new and used items, so it's a good place to start. Check off items listed below as you complete them. I have more details on these checklist items throughout the book.

1. Plan

☐ Decide how much money you can spend on supplies and inventory to start

☐ Determine how much you need to make in order for this to be worthwhile

☐ Decide the name of your business

☐ Will you incorporate or just use a DBA to start? (DBA="Doing Business As")

☐ You do not need to decide now if you want to incorporate, but make a note to yourself to think about it later. You may want to read the *Inc. and Grow Rich* book listed in the "Resources" chapter at the end of the book

2. Set up your business

☐ Get your desired DBA from your state. Texas has an online database you can search to be sure the business name you want is available; then you pay a small fee to "own" it for 10 years

☐ Go online to www.irs.gov and request a business tax ID number in the name of your DBA or corporation. Your business does not have to be incorporated to get this number. You can even get one in your name, although this is not recommended

☐ File for your state sales tax number (you can do it online in most states) so you can buy merchandise tax-free

☐ Open a separate checking account for your business. It does not have to be a business checking account per se, but needs to be separate from your personal account(s) for tax purposes and for ease of accounting. Many banks (like Chase), allow you to set up accounts online

☐ Sign up for a UPS business account online using your business tax ID and DBA

☐ Review Amazon's latest fees and set up a spreadsheet to help you determine your break-even point and minimum selling prices

3. Order supplies. Depending on your beginning resources, order/source these supplies. The first four are critical to start. See chapters 3, 8 and the "Resources" section at the end of this book for specifics on where to get these items

☐ USB hand-held scanner that plugs into a USB port on your computer

☐ Shipping boxes (18"x12"x12" or smaller works well for books)

☐ Packing tape and paper (or bubble wrap or air pillows – NO foam peanuts)

☐ Free UPS shipping labels (two per 8.5"x11" page). You need to sign up and then wait about 3-4 days until you can place your first order

☐ Dymo LabelWriter 450 Turbo printer (or a Zebra printer). If you already have a printer capable of printing rolls of adhesive labels up to 2"x3" in size, that is worth testing with FBAPower. Dymo and Zebra are the two that I know for sure work

☐ Address-sized labels for your Dymo printer (they can range from 1"x2" to 2"x3" in size)

☐ Smartphone (FBAScout runs on phones with the Android operating system and Apple iPhone phones). Amazon.com sells cell phones as low as one penny with a two-year contract. Be sure to check that out if you need a smartphone. For a while, Virgin was offering terrific prices on Android monthly subscription fees – around $40 a month – so be sure to shop around

☐ Scanfob Bluetooth™ scanner to use with your smartphone

☐ Lanyard or string for Scanfob

☐ Protective carrier for your Smartphone. (I use an armband/wristband)

☐ Shipping scale that calculates weights up to at least 75 lbs

4. Round up your inventory from around the house

☐ Books

☐ DVDs

☐ CDs

☐ Video games

☐ VHS tapes

☐ Software with packaging in good shape

☐ Anything new, still sealed in its original packaging

5. Set up your Amazon seller account and FBAPower

☐ See Chapter 10 for step-by-step instructions

☐ Scan, price and label your items

☐ "Ship" your items from FBAPower to Amazon Seller Central™

6. Send in your first shipment

☐ See Chapter 11

☐ Pack and weigh your box(es)

☐ Go through the 7-step shipment process on Seller Central

☐ Take your box(es) to a UPS drop site or arrange a pick-up

7. Go shopping for more inventory

☐ Set up your Scanfob and Smartphone. See Chapter 12

☐ Determine the locations of your local Big Lots, Toys "R" Us, Dollar General, TJMaxx, Marshall's, Tuesday Morning, Target, Wal-Mart (and so on), thrift stores, and library branches. See Chapter 16 for ideas of where to find inventory

☐ Find out about local book sales by calling your library branches or looking at their "Friends" sites online, checking out newspapers and looking at sites like these: www.booksalefinder.com, www.booksalemanager.com

☐ Look for garage and estate sales that advertise lots of books

☐ Note all local church/temple rummage sales in your calendar as they occur

throughout the year – they'll occur about the same time again next year

Cynthia Stine

5

WHAT CAN I SELL ON AMAZON?

You can sell just about anything with a barcode on Amazon – toys, games, home goods, bedding, books, computers, software, electronics, pet supplies, tools, food, appliances and much, much more. There are several categories of restricted goods. Some of them (like clothing and guns) require permission from Amazon first and others (like porn) simply cannot be sold on the site . Some categories, like toys and games, are NOT restricted if you are an FBA seller, but are restricted during the holiday season if you are a merchant seller. This is because Amazon handles the fulfillment and controls the customer experience; Amazon is obsessed with providing a good experience for its customers. Being able to sell toys at Christmas without restriction is another big benefit to being an FBA seller.

Restricted items:
- Hazardous materials
- Certain batteries
- Certain liquids
- Live animals
- Items that weigh more than 150 lbs
- Pornographic materials

You can sell in these categories as soon as you sign up:
- Baby
- Books*
- Camera & Photo
- DVDs*
- Electronics
- Everything Else
- Grocery
- Health & Personal Care
- Home & Garden
- Music*
- Musical Instruments
- Office Products
- Software
- Sports & Outdoors
- Tools & Home Improvement
- Toys & Games

- Video Games
- Videos*

* You will only be able to list these products to the extent that Amazon makes available functionality to list such products. In other words, you can sell books but not magazines, CDs but not MP3 files – that kind of thing. There are several places where you can find all these rules and exceptions: 1) your contract. Print it off and read it more than once; 2) on Seller Central in Amazon (look under "help") and; 3) in the FBA Manual also found in Seller Central. You'll want to refer to this a lot in the beginning.

You can submit a request to Amazon to sell in these categories. Read the rules first. Many simply require you to have been a seller with Amazon for a certain amount of time. Others – like Collectible Books – require a special knowledge or expertise in the category in order to sell:

- Clothing & Accessories
- Automotive Parts, Motorcycle & ATV
- Beauty
- Cell Phones & Accessories
- Collectible Books
- Gourmet Food
- Jewelry
- Personal Computers

- Shoes
- Watches

This list is by no means comprehensive. You can find a complete list through your Amazon Seller Central account [look under the "FBA Manual" under "Help"]. Be sure to check the list if you are entering a new category as the rules might have changed since the last time you looked. For example, Amazon now allows its FBA Sellers to sell non-media overseas, so I expect there will be even more rule changes.

Currently you can sell all your media on overseas Amazon sites. This includes books, DVDs, videos, CDs, video games and software. Once your seller account is established [see instructions later in the book to set up your seller account], it is very easy to arrange to sell media internationally. Under the "Inventory" tab in Seller Central, go to the "Inventory Amazon Fulfills" page. There is a button to click to sell internationally. You will be required to send in a PDF of your signature for their records and that's it! Now your media listings will be visible on several international sites.

My books are better traveled than I am. I sold a book to someone in Sofia, Bulgaria once.

One caveat to keep in mind is that with the exception of media, Amazon insists that items for sale be new. For most collectibles, used clothing, etc., you'll want to use eBay. Amazon has also returned items to me that were damaged in the warehouse; I was then able to sell these items on eBay or Craigslist with a picture and an explanation that it was brand new with a slightly damaged box.

TAKE ACTION!

- Read all the categories on Amazon's website
- Spend time looking at the top sellers in each category to get a feel for them
- Determine which categories are most appealing to you and make sure you understand any requirements or restrictions
- For your chosen categories, create a spreadsheet of your own to help you understand your margins and minimum pricing. If you are selling something heavy, like tools or cans of food, be sure to adjust for the extra shipping costs

Cynthia Stine

6

IS IT HARD TO FIND INVENTORY?

Finding inventory is the easiest part of this business. There is more potential inventory than I can possibly buy with my budget. Almost everywhere I turn, there are opportunities. For this reason, it is very important to have a specific budget and criteria in mind when shopping, or else you can spend like crazy.

<u>Thrift stores</u> – There are hundreds of thrift stores in my area and I've barely explored them because the ones I've visited have been so good that I run out of money before I run out of opportunities. Generally, I find books, videos, CDs, audio books and – sometimes – -new toys still sealed in their boxes. Often there are special sales dates that are worth noting. For example, one thrift store I mentioned earlier offers 20-cent hardbacks and 10-cent paperbacks on Saturdays between 10 a.m. and 2 p.m.

<u>Book sales</u> – Spring and fall are the biggest seasons for book sales. There are several kinds: library book sales, warehouse sales/auctions, retail book sales and other book sales. Usually a book sale is to support a group or charity. Big sales will often be listed on book sale websites like www.booksalefinder.com or www.booksalemanager.com.

In addition, libraries have societies called "Friends of the Library" that usually host the annual book sale(s). These sales can be at the branch level or for a whole library system. We have both types of sales in the Metroplex where I live. Arlington, for example, has one big library sale twice a year for all its branches, while Dallas lets each branch host its own. If you can't find information on the library branch website, call them.

Prices at these sales tend to be 25 cents for videos, $1-$2 for DVDs and CDs, 50 cents to $1 for paperbacks and $1-$2 for hardbacks. Often there is a small fee to become a friend of the library, which is well worth it because it gives you advance notice of the sales and early entry into the sale. Universities sometimes also have book sales as do charitable groups like the local ASPCA.

<u>Warehouse sales and auctions</u> are often announced in the newspaper and are for large lots of books. These books may have been acquired as lost property (think of the postal service or the airport)

when the owner could not be found, or may be from a retail store looking to get rid of poor-performing merchandise or perhaps going out of business like Borders did in 2011. Sometimes a large library book sale will sell off the remainders to the highest bidder at the end of the sale. I just bought approximately 30,000 books from a library book sale with two friends of mine. We feel a bit like the dog that caught the car as we prepare to sort and process them in a four-to-five-month period, working our Amazon businesses part-time.

Retail stores will often have ongoing sale tables in addition to big sales a few times a year. In North Texas, we have Half Price Books, which has fabulous sales with discounts off their already low prices. In November 2011, they had a warehouse sale for the first time and everything was $3 or less. Barnes & Noble regularly has discount sections and sale tables. Stores like Wal-Mart, Sam's Club, Target and others also sell books and media – just keep an eye out for clearance items. Big Lots has books from 25 cents and up. It's a mixed bag there – I've learned the hard way that a lot of other FBA sellers shop at Big Lots and sometimes it takes me months to clear multiples of books bought there.

At my local Blockbuster Video, I bought a few books that shouldn't have been there in the first place. They were brand new and sold nicely online. The lesson to me was to look around everywhere I go and to bring my scanner.

To find out about sales, I get on as many mail/email lists as possible. It means setting up folders in my Outlook email box to handle the deluge of email, but it is worth it. If you go to a book sale, be sure to get on their mailing list for next time (usually by becoming a "friend," but not always).

Ongoing library book sales are slightly different from other book sales in that they are going on all the time. The library generally has a room or alcove where there are books for sale and you can go any time to shop. New books come in as donations are made, or as the library clears its shelves. In Dallas, the downtown public library has a permanent "bookstore" inside the library. In addition to the prices listed daily, once a month they sell books for $5 a box (bring your own box). Fort Worth has a similar arrangement. In addition to the ongoing sale, the Fort Worth library also has big annual sales, with even more heavily discounted prices, that it advertises to the public. You can find out about these ongoing sales either at the book sale finder websites (see "resources" at the end of the book), on your library's website, or by calling the main branches of the libraries in your area.

Discount stores like Big Lots tend to get books in huge lots that are basically overstocks. Scan with care to make sure you are not competing with a bunch of other FBA sellers. Other discount stores like Dollar Tree and the Dollar Store have yielded finds. The great thing about buying at a retail store is that the book/video game/CD/DVD is new and more likely to get you a higher price. Wal-Mart, Sam's, Costco and others will quickly clear out a book or media item that is not selling fast enough for their business model. These media items are often still quite popular and can be good sellers for you.

Discount stores are also a great source of new toys, games and other merchandise to sell on Amazon. I've shopped Marshall's, TJ Maxx, Tuesday Morning, Target, Wal-Mart, Kmart and a few specialty shops over the past year with good results.

Other Amazon sellers sometimes sell books for ridiculously low prices. Often these mistakes come from not understanding how to use their repricer. If you see a hot book (possibly because you want to sell it yourself) selling for one penny or even $1 FBA, it may make sense to buy it and then re-sell it. Someone is going to buy that book, and might as well be you. (This strategy assumes you are a Prime member and will get free shipping on the item.) Most sellers only need to make a mistake like that once or twice before they fix the problem with their inventory repricer.

Other sources of inventory include estate sales, storage unit auctions and many more. Although I've not yet ventured into these areas, there is a good book on this topic listed in the resources section. If you are like me, you'll have more opportunities than money in the beginning so you won't need to branch out until your business is bigger.

TAKE ACTION!

- Go to Google Maps and search for Big Lots, Wal-Mart, Target, etc. to find out which retailers are near you
- Do another search for thrift stores in a five-mile radius. Create a driving map for yourself so you can check them out efficiently when you are ready. Increase your radius as needed until you have at least five stores to explore
- Check out www.booksalefinder.com and www.booksalemanager.com to find book sales in your area. Also, start keeping a calendar of books sales as you find them – many sales are not on these lists
- Find the nearest library to you as well as the city's main branch and determine how they run their book sales and when the next one(s) will be. Do the same for other nearby cities

7

DOES IT TAKE A LOT OF TIME?

On average, I spend about 10 hours a week on my Amazon business. In reality, it is more like 40 hours a month spent in big bursts. I may go to a big book sale or on a shopping trip and then spend a few more hours boxing things up and sending to Amazon. Afterward, I might do nothing for a couple of weeks aside from some repricing. The flexibility of this business is one of its more appealing facets. Here's my hours breakout:

- One-time up-front learning and set-up: about 15-20 hours, depending on your level of comfort with technology and how much reading you want to do in advance
  - Amazon Seller set-up
  - FBA set-up
  - Upload and scouting tools
  - Books to read (see resources)

* Supply acquisition: 1 hour every few months to drive to Uline (a store that stocks packing and mailing supplies) for more boxes
* Inventory acquisition: 3-4 hours a week depending on my schedule
* Preparing shipments to Amazon: 5-6 hours a week, depending on number of boxes
* Re-pricing: 1-2 hours as needed, about once or twice a month
* Tax/bookkeeping: ongoing, a few hours a month

I already have a business that I own so my time to set up the business legally and with a tax ID was zero. I am using a DBA ("doing business as") that I already own, and I'm running the Amazon business and its accounting through my current corporate entity. If you are not incorporated yet, I suggest you do so for legal and tax reasons that are quite profitable. If you at least have a DBA, you will be able to get a sales tax certificate, which in Texas saves me 8.25% on purchases. You will also be able to open up a business bank account, which I highly recommend, and pay your taxes like a corporation (i.e., _after_ all expenses have been paid) instead of as an individual (_before_ paying for expenses).

Since my business was already incorporated in Texas and I have other businesses here, I didn't pursue other options. If this is your only business, you may want to consider incorporating in Nevada. It is an excellent state for online resellers for several reasons:

1. Extreme privacy laws provide better protection for you as an individual.
2. Low population, which means your number of Nevada customers will be small and thus your sales tax (paid only for sales to customers in the same state as your business) will be small.
3. Inexpensive incorporation and PO Box services available to keep you legally a Nevada corporation.

Just so you know, your business does not need to be in the same state in which you live if it is a business that sells nationwide. There are several good resources to consult regarding incorporation, including Inc. and Grow Rich [http://amzn.to/incandgrow], which has helped me enormously the past 17 years.

If you look at my sales numbers for last year, you'll see that there were months during which I barely worked my Amazon business and others during which I worked a lot more than 40 hours a month. Your business will do better the more time you can give it, of course, but the real question to ask yourself is whether it will perform well enough *in the time you have to give.*

TAKE ACTION!

- If you haven't already, get incorporated and secure any DBA(s) you want to use with your business
- You can get a DBA even if you are not incorporated. Because incorporation can take a few weeks, go ahead and get your DBA first and use it to register with Amazon and to set up a bank account. In many states you can search DBAs online to determine if the one you want is already taken – much like going to "Go Daddy" to see if a URL is available. Then you can register in person or mail in the paperwork to secure your DBA
- Open a bank account for business use only
- Get your sales tax certificate from the state in which you are incorporated. In Texas, most of the paperwork can be done online

8

WHAT DO I NEED TO MAKE IT WORK?

I wrote this chapter for the reader who skipped to this question. You sequential readers will find parts of it repetitive.

You can start this business very modestly and work your way up. Here are the tools I use to run my business today. I note which ones are necessary from the beginning and which can be added later as you have more money. I had less than $200 to start with and had to wait to buy certain tools. My Dad, who has credit cards and more capital, was able to start with everything he needed right from the beginning.

To list on Amazon:
- Handheld USB scanner – almost any kind will do. Amazon sells several for under $30. They plug into a USB port on your

computer and allow you to scan ISBN and UPC codes into your computer. You can type in the codes manually, but using a scanner is much faster and easier.

- FBAPower – www.fbapower.com. The first two weeks are free. Click on http://bit.ly/2freeweeks and you'll get an additional two weeks free for a total of a month. After that, it is $39.95 a month.

To ship to Amazon:

- LabelWriter Turbo 450 or Zebra label printer – To print labels as you go. Because Amazon will print labels for you for free, on 8.5"x11" sheets (30 to a page), you can wait on this if need be.
- Labels – No need to buy brand name labels; get the cheapest you can that are address size. My labels cost me less than half a penny each.
- Packing tape – I recommend 3 tape so you can cover all seams in one swipe. Uline (www.uline.com) sells tape by the case and gives you a free industrial tape dispenser to go with it. Some people, particularly those with small children, prefer the "silent" tape, but it costs more.

- **Boxes** – Book sales will often have lots of good book boxes lying around, which will help offset your costs, but you'll still need to buy some boxes new. I buy from Uline, which has a warehouse near me so I don't pay shipping costs. I get my boxes (18x12x12) for 90 cents when I buy 25.

- **Packing paper or bubble wrap** – To date I've not had to buy any because I had a supply in my garage, and I get more as things are mailed to me. Amazon is particular as to what they will let you use as filler (no foam peanuts, for example), so be sure to read their shipping instructions carefully. I'm planning to buy some clean newsprint from Uline the next time I go.

- **UPS account** – Free. You need it so you can get free adhesive shipping labels and arrange pick-ups of large orders. The labels you need are on 8.5"x11" paper (two labels per sheet) that feeds into your printer. You will need one sheet per box that you ship. Generally, UPS will send you 50 sheets at a time, delivered to your door for free. You can also print labels on paper in a pinch, but adhesive labels are better.

You will also need a UPS account if you plan to have shipments picked up at your house. I do this when I have a lot of boxes, especially toy boxes that are much bigger and harder to fit in my car. It costs anywhere from $6 to $9 for a UPS pick-up, depending on fuel surcharges. This is a flat fee regardless of the number of boxes and is an excellent service for big shipments. You do NOT need a UPS account to ship to Amazon because you will be using Amazon's account. More on this later.

* Black permanent marker pen – Can't live without this. I use it to mark my book boxes at book sales and to help me weigh and mark my book boxes at home.
* Scale – I started with my bathroom scale. Eventually you'll want a digital scale designed for packages, with a flat top. It is hard to stand on a scale with a 50-pound box and get an accurate read. I bought a WeighMax [http://amzn.to/weighmax] digital scale on Amazon for about $20. It weighs packages up to 75 lbs., which is plenty because you are not supposed to ship boxes heavier than 50 lbs to Amazon.

To scout for inventory:

* Scanfob – This is the Bluetooth scanner I use for scouting. It costs approximately $350 although you can get a discount code from Chris Green's site to buy it for about $282. Obviously if you don't have the money for it now, save up for it. In the meantime, you can scan barcodes into your smart phone using the camera on your phone or read them in using the voice entry feature. It is slower, but free. Other Bluetooth scanners are available and may be less expensive. I am not familiar with these other scanners, but FBAScout will work with any Bluetooth scanner that will work with your phone. I like my Scanfob because I can scan from a fair distance from the item. I am short and many interesting boxes are on top shelves so I find that feature useful.

* FBAScout – Free for the first 250 scans so you can see if you like it, then a monthly subscription fee of $39.95. (The application itself is free.) If you are also an FBAPower customer, you get a bundled price of $59.95 for both services. You will want this once you start scouting in earnest. There is nothing like it on the market – it is the only

program that shows you FBA offers as well as new and used prices. It also tells you how many units the other sellers have and what your net from Amazon will be at a certain price point. It is a crucial tool for my business.

- Smartphone – FBAScout runs on iPhone, iPad, iPod touch and phones with Android. As long as you have one of these devices, you can scout with FBAScout. I was able to get my Android phone from Amazon (yes, they sell cellular service too!) for one penny when I extended my AT&T service for an additional two years. They even delivered my phone overnight. It is one heck of a deal. I then sold my iPhone on Craigslist. This was before the iPhone version of FBAScout was available.
- Armband/wristband – I use this to hold and protect my phone, and free up my hands. It is about $8 at Amazon. Not critical, of course, but helpful.

Other tools:
- FBARepricer – This comes with FBAPower and you get ten repricings a month for free. If you want to do more, there is a subscription fee. Due to my time

restrictions, I'm lucky if I can reprice more than once or twice a month so I use the free service.

- Excel – Most Amazon reports and the repricer export data into a format that is opened by Excel. If you are not familiar with Excel, you will need to spend some time learning the basics of how to sort data and move data around in a spreadsheet. Other spreadsheet programs may also be able to open these files as well.
- Un-du label remover – A solvent for those darned sticky price labels that Big Lots and other retailers put on their products. I now buy it in bulk at Uline.com, but you can find it online or at office supply stores. A little goes a long way and it works great without damaging the packaging. Other sellers swear by Goof-Off, but I found it doesn't work so well with the Big Lots stickers (they are heinous).
- Scotty Peelers – A miracle for peeling off labels. The peelers get under the label and lift it off.

TAKE ACTION!

- Look at this list and take note of items you may already have and items you need to get started.At a minimum you will want a scanner, shipping labels from UPS and sheet labels (for pricing) for your printer

- This list assumes you have a computer with internet access and a printer. If you don't have these items, think about whose equipment you might be able to borrow or share until you can buy your own
- Is your phone a smartphone? If not, get one
- Do you have packing materials? If not, you may be able to get materials for free or very cheap on Craigslist (from people moving, etc.). Just be sure the boxes are still strong enough for books and the packing paper is clean (no newsprint)

9

HOW MUCH DOES IT COST TO GET STARTED?

As I mentioned earlier in the book, I started out Spartan. I bought a USB scanner (about $30), a LabelWriter 450 Turbo with labels (about $110 in all), 25 book boxes ($25) and a crate of tape (about $50). I packed up and shipped books from my shelves. I got a free month with FBAPower and determined to make the most of it.

I signed up with Amazon, which cost me $39.99 a month but I didn't have pay that until a few weeks later when I was already making money. I sent boxes to Amazon, which did not cost me shipping up front.

Once I went through my inventory and made some money, I was ready to scout for new inventory. I rented ASellerTool's PDA solution off eBay because renting was cheaper than buying at the time. ASellerTool still cost me about $345 to get started but I got $285 back later when I returned the PDA. I also had a monthly subscription fee of $44.95 with ASellerTool for the data. As I said, it was the best deal around at the time. FBAScout is much cheaper to get started.

When FBAScout came out late in 2010, I returned the ASellerTool hardware and used my deposit return to buy the Scanfob 2002 ($282). I started using the Scanfob and FBAScout in December 2010 and it made a huge difference in my business. Along the way, as I made money I put some back into inventory, some toward my family and some toward things like the digital scale, more boxes, more labels, etc.

So, to answer the question of how much does it cost to get started – as little as $200 and as much as $640 plus inventory and shipping costs:

Item	Cost
USB Scanner	$30
LabelWriter 450 Turbo	$90
Labels	$20
Boxes	$25
Tape	$50

FBAPower (first month free)	$39.95 ($59.95 bundle with FBAScout)/month
FBAScout (250 scans free)	$39.95/month or bundle
Digital Scale	$22.50
Scanfob	$280
Smartphone	$.01 (with a 2-year commitment)
Un-du	$8-$10
Armband/wristband smartphone holder	$10-$12
Amazon Pro Seller account	$39.99/month
Shipping	50 cents a pound, roughly

TAKE ACTION!

* Determine your starting budget
* Order/pick up your supplies
* See if there is a Uline warehouse near you. If not, you will probably need to source your boxes, tape, etc. somewhere else because shipping from Uline can be high. Look for a wholesaler/warehouse in your area. It may be advantageous to take a trip to Atlanta, Chicago,

Dallas, etc., to get supplies a few times a year. Also, check out Wal-Mart. Some sellers have found good prices on boxes there

- If you want to start small, your local office supply superstore should have what you need as well – it will cost more per unit, but you can get a roll of tape for $4 rather than $50 for a case

10

READY? SET...

Don't read this chapter until you are in front of your computer and ready to set up your Amazon Pro Seller account and FBAPower. This is very hands-on.

OK, now to get started! In addition to setting up your accounts, I will walk you through your first shipment to Amazon in this chapter. Chapter 11 will get you set up with FBAScout.

I have borrowed liberally from the FBAPower website for some of these screen shots. There is an excellent step-by-step guide on the website, but it is not always easy to find. Plus, it is hard to switch back and forth between screens when you're trying to get setup, so I'm going to give you the web link: http://www.fbapower.com/guide/step1.html *and* cover it below.

Sign up on Amazon:

First you need to sign up for a Pro Seller account. FBAPower does not work with a basic seller account. Please note that you cannot have more than one seller account so if you are already selling on Amazon, you will need to login and upgrade to a Pro Seller account instead. If you are already a Pro Seller, you can ignore this step.

1. Go to <u>www.sellercentral.amazon.com</u>
2. Click on "Register now" near the bottom
3. On the next page on the lower right-hand side you will see "Sell Professionally" and the "Start Selling" button. Click to the next page

4. You will need the following information:
   a. Your business name, address, and contact information
   b. An internationally-chargeable debit or credit card with valid billing address
   c. A phone number where you can be reached during this registration process
5. You want to create a <u>new account</u> rather than use your personal account with Amazon. Remember, you can only have *one* selling account with Amazon
6. Fill in the forms and continue the registration process

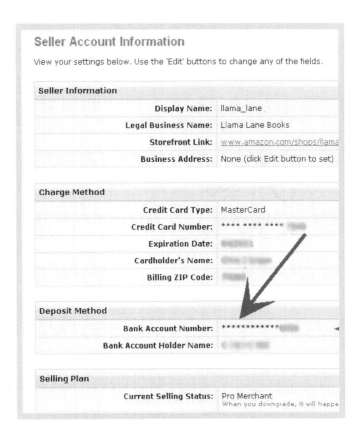

7. Next, sign up for Amazon's FBA program at: http://www.amazonservices.com/content/fulfillment-by-amazon.htm#features-and-benefits

8. Be sure to sign up with the *same* email and password you used to sign up as a Pro Seller

9. There are four numbers you will need to capture for your FBAPower account. Be sure to cut and paste them into a word document for later use and some will be quite long

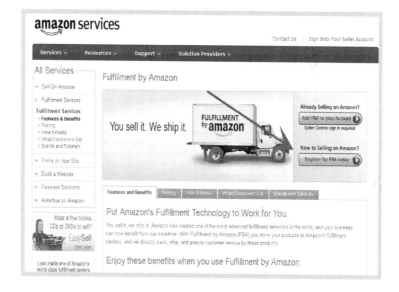

10. Next, go to: http://aws.amazon.com/fws/ and sign up

11. Once you've signed up, you will come to a screen like the one below. Click on "Resource Center"

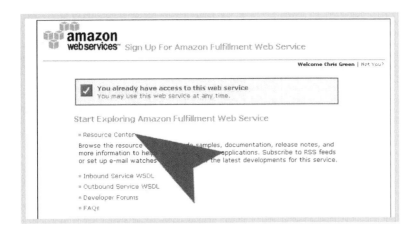

12. On the Resource Center page, click on "Account"

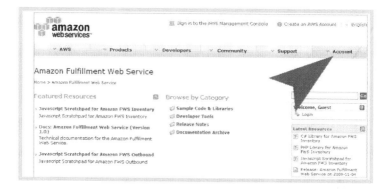

13. On the next page, click on "Security Credentials"

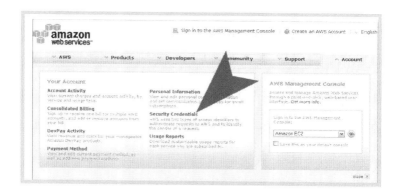

14. On the next page, you will need to cut and paste some numbers. I strongly suggest you cut and paste them into a separate document and save them because you will likely need them again

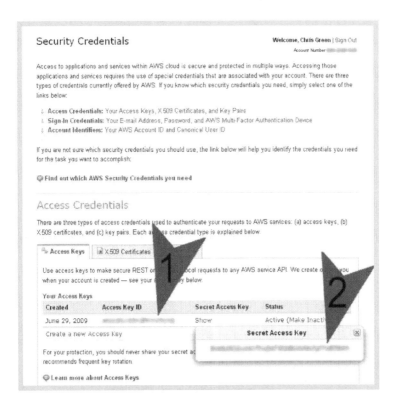

15. Capture your "Access Key ID" and your "Secret Access Key"

16. Next, you will need to sign up for an "MWS" account with Amazon at: https://developer.amazonservices.com/. Once these accounts are all set up, you'll rarely think about them again

17. You will be asked to log in. Once again, be sure to use the same email and

password you used for your Pro Seller account

18. Once you are signed up and logged in, click on "I want to use an application...." Then input the following information from FBAPower:

a. Application name: FBAPower
b. Developer Account Number: 6771-7968-3933

19. Click on "next." You will be taken to a screen where you give Amazon permission for FBAPower to access your data. Agree to everything and click "next"

20. Be sure to print off your license agreement and keep it for future reference

21. Success! You will now have more numbers to cut and paste – your Merchant ID# and your Marketplace ID#. Please note these will never be emailed to you. The only way to get these numbers is by logging in

22. **Either as you go or later, be sure to print off your Pro Seller and FBA contracts. There is a lot of good information in the contracts that you will want to read again later. I have mine in a 3-ring-binder for handy reference**

Set up FBAPower:

1. **Once you have your seller account set up, you will need to set up your FBAPower account. You will need specific information from your Amazon seller account to make it work. FBAPower works best with the Firefox browser**

(free) so I suggest you download it if you don't already have it on your system: www.firefox.com. Sign up for the free one-month FBAPower trial at http://bit.ly/2freeweeks

2.   As a reminder, here are the four items you collected from your seller account. Be sure to cut and paste the data into a secure file. You might need the information again in the future:

3.

    a.   Access Key ID_____

    b.   Secret Access Key_____

    c.   Merchant ID_____

    d.   Marketplace ID_____

4.   Log in to your FBAPower account and click on "account" in the upper right-hand corner

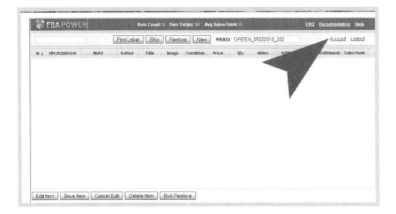

5. You will go to a screen that looks like this:

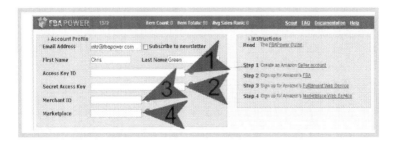

6. Fill in the numbers you collected from Amazon

7. That's it! You are now ready to use FBAPower

8. In the next chapter, I will talk about changing your settings and using FBAPower. Chris Green has several excellent videos on his site about his product and how it works. Before we go to

the next step, I strongly encourage you to scroll down to the bottom of the page on this link: http://www.fbapower.com/what-is-fba-power/about/ and read about FBAPower. I also strongly recommend that you watch all of Chris' videos on this link: http://www.fbapower.com/what-is-fba-power/videos/. You will see Chris in action, using the product in a way that words can't adequately describe

TAKE ACTION!

- Set up your Amazon and FBAPower accounts
- Print off all your contracts and *read* them. Amazon expects you to know this information and not knowing it can get you into trouble
- Watch all the videos on the FBAPower site about how to use FBAPower
- Get your books and supplies together in readiness for the next step – your first shipment to Amazon

Cynthia Stine

11

GO! YOUR FIRST BOX TO AMAZON

Are your accounts set up on Amazon and FBAPower? Then it is time to start listing and pricing your inventory! For simplicity's sake, start with a box of the same type of items (books or CDs or DVDs or video games, for example) so that everything will be going to the same warehouse. Your box cannot weigh more than 50 pounds when it is shipped, so figure on between 35 and 50 books per box depending on size and type.

Here's what you will accomplish in this chapter:

1. Set up your USB scanner
2. Set up your label printer if you have one
3. Adjust your settings in FBAPower
4. Set up a naming and numbering system for your inventory
5. List a box of books
6. Pack and ship your box to Amazon

Set up your USB scanner

Plug your hand-held scanner into one of the USB ports on your computer. With some scanners, this is all you need to do--your system will automatically download all the drivers, etc. For other systems, you may need to read the directions. Most scanners come with a page of different bar codes and numbers. These are test pages and many of the weird-looking ones are for highly specialized applications that you will never use, so ignore them. What you want to do is test your scanner on an ISBN #.

1. Open up a word processing file (in MS Word or whatever program you use) and place your cursor at the top of the page.
2. Place the test paper that came with the scanner on your desk and scan from your test sheet.
3. You should hear a beep of some kind and a string of numbers will appear at the top of your screen.
4. Grab a book and scan the ISBN # to test the scanner. If the number appears at the top of your word processing page, it is working.

With hand-held scanners, you generally have to get pretty close to the item being scanned. With the Bluetooth scanner that you'll use for scouting, you can be far away from the barcode.

Once you are comfortable that your scanner is working, move on to the label printer.

Set up label printer

If you don't have a label printer yet, skip to the next section. I'm going to cover the highlights here, but the FBAPower site is quite comprehensive. There is a video at http://bit.ly/printersettings that covers setting up your printer as well. You may want to watch it first.

1. First, make sure your label printer is plugged into a USB port on your computer and to the electrical outlet.

2. Load a roll of labels into the printer. The waxy side of the label should be up and the label should be facing down as you feed it through the slot.

3. The printer may load its own drivers from the Internet or you may need to use the DVD that came with it to get it properly installed on your computer or network.

4. Once your label printer is working, you will need tell it two things and then print a test label. I'll show you below what everything should look like when you're set up properly:

    a. The orientation of the label (landscape)

    b. The number of the label you will be using

5. Make sure you are using Firefox as your browser. It is a free download if you don't already have it [www.firefox.com].

6. Go to http://www.fbapower.com/fba-forums/printer-setup-pc/ (or http://www.fbapower.com/fba-forums/printer-setup-mac/ if you are a Mac user).

7. If you are a Mac user, your screens will be similar but not the same as shown below. I don't use a Mac, so I can't screen-capture for you, but FBAPower has all the instructions and screen shots at http://www.fbapower.com/fba-forums/printer-setup-mac/.

8. Click on the test label link, or put this address in your Firefox browser window: http://fbapower.com/testlabel/index.php.htm.

9. The screen should look like this:

10. Go under "File" at the top left-hand side of your browser screen and choose "Print Preview."

11. Next, click on "print." Make sure to choose your label printer.

12. Then click on "properties."

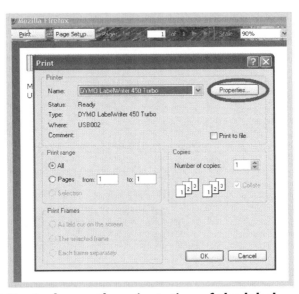

13. Next, choose the orientation of the label (Landscape) and go to the advanced settings.

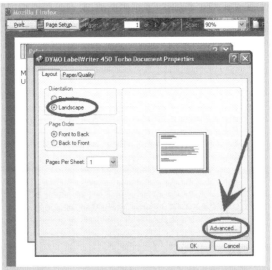

14. Under "Advanced," choose your particular label. Amazon allows for several similar sizes of address labels. Pick yours from this list. 30336 is common, as is 30252 or 30320.

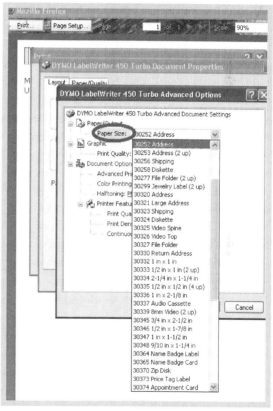

15. You are almost ready to print your test strip. Save your settings and go back to the "print preview" screen.

16. Click on "Page Setup."

17. You want to make sure to select "Landscape" for orientation. *Don't* make any changes to "Scale" or "Shrink to fit Page Width" yet. You may need to adjust these later, but first go to "Margins and Header/Footer."

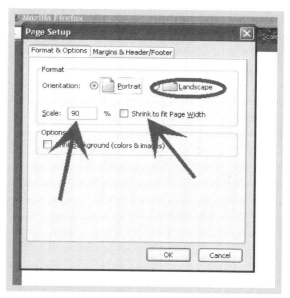

18. You want all your settings on this screen to look like this.

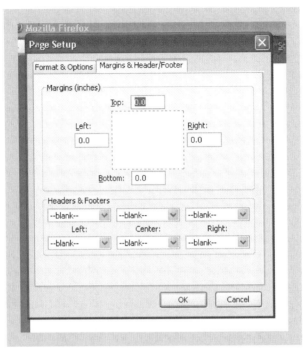

19. If anything is different on your screen, change it until it looks like this with all zeros and "blanks."

20. Click "OK" when you are done and go back to the "Print Preview" screen.

21. Print a label.

22. If the label looks good, you are done. If the print is too big or too small for the label, you will need to go back to the "Formats and Options" screen and adjust your settings until the label prints correctly.

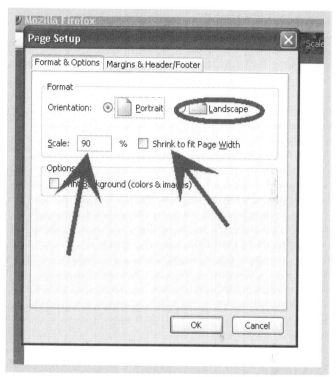

23. Adjust and print labels until you are satisfied. You want to make sure the entire text of the label prints, not just the barcode. The two settings in the picture above are the ones that will make the difference.

24. Leave the Firefox tab with the test strip open and click on a new tab to open a new screen.

25. Login to your FBAPower account at www.fbapower.com

You may find yourself having to adjust your printer settings from time to time in the future for no particular reason that I can figure out. As long as you know that, you won't panic. Most of the time, all that's needed is to re-select the correct label number you are using and fix the orientation to landscape. Sometimes you have to go through the whole process and adjust the margins and header/footer as well.

Adjust your settings in FBAPower

Now you are ready to start using FBAPower to list your inventory and ship it to Amazon's warehouse(s). (In addition to the steps below, I highly recommend that you watch FBAPower's specific video on FBAPower settings at http://bit.ly/fbaaccountsetting.) Next, click on the "Account" link.

1. "Account" is where you can change your settings. For this first batch, you may choose to use the default settings, which is what I did with my first few shipments. Over time, I changed them to reflect my inventory. The whole idea here is to _automate_ repetitive activities. So, for

example, if you have a lot of library books and find yourself writing notes that your book has library stickers on it, you may choose to change a setting so you don't have to keep typing the same thing over and over.

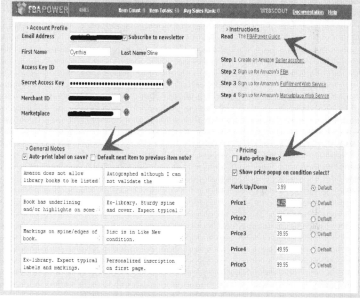

2. First, note the FBAPower guide in the upper right-hand corner. Return to this if you have questions later.

3. "General Notes" are *optional* notes that you choose. These notes will be made available to you as clickable notes on the listing screen. You will see that your notes are different from mine because I've made

changes over time to reflect my inventory. You can change these at any time. For example, if you have a big shipment of CDs/DVDs, you might want some general notes relating to disc condition and jewel cases. I have a separate word file with all the notes I've used over the past year. This way I can simply cut and paste depending on my inventory. When processing inventory, I tend to lump "like" things together (books, CDs, DVDs, toys, etc.) for faster processing.

4. FBAPower has given you notes to start with. If you click on any of the notes, you'll be able to read the full text and to change it if desired.

5. "Auto-print label on save" means that once you choose a note on the listing screen, the print label screen will pop up.

6. "Default next item to previous item note" is great when your inventory is mostly the same. For example, if you have many used library books to process, you might want that default option so you don't have to keep clicking on the note that says "Ex-library..." Most of the time I leave this setting off.

7. Under "pricing," you have the option to let the program suggest a price for you. You may want to do that in the beginning as a mental exercise. For example, you might ask yourself "I wonder why it suggested that price?" I prefer to set my own prices so I have it unchecked. Whether this option is checked or not, <u>you can always set your own price</u> on the listing page.

8. "Show price popup" should be checked because it speeds the flow of processing your items.

9. Prices 1-5 are completely up to you. These prices are available to you when pricing your item, so you can click on the price and move on. Again, if you have inventory items that are very similar, this is a great idea. OR if you would like reminders of your price floor, use this function.

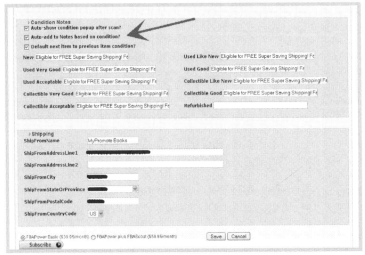

10. Here is the bottom part of the "Account" screen.

11. "Condition Notes" are automatically filled in for you when you select a condition for your merchandise. You can edit this to anything you like. For now, I suggest you leave it as is.

12. Amazon has very particular criteria for condition. It is part of your contract with them and I suggest you <u>read it carefully</u>. Library books, for example, can never be sold for any condition better than "good" even if they are in pristine condition. That's why I have notes about library books so I can communicate better to my customers about the actual condition of the book and

what they can expect when they get it. You don't want unhappy customers so it is important that you are accurate in setting your conditions. It is better to be a bit conservative than to be too liberal in your interpretations. Think about how YOU would feel if you got this book in the mail.

13. For the three check boxes, I normally keep the first two checked, but not the third unless, again, I've sorted my inventory such that the condition will be the same for most of the books. You can always manually change settings on the listing page. I recently processed a batch of library books that were all in "good" condition, so I checked the third box.

14. Now, click on "Save" and let's go list your books!

Set up a numbering and naming system for your inventory

FBAPower has several helpful videos about its product that I strongly suggest you watch before you start listing inventory. One video explains batches (http://bit.ly/batchvideo) and another explains how to create a listing (http://bit.ly/fbaspeedtest).

You'll get to see how fast processing your inventory goes once you are set up. I generally process between 50 and 60 unique items an hour and sometimes more. This first shipment will take you the longest because you are learning, but very soon, you'll easily be able to fill and ship a box an hour.

Amazon requires that you have a unique identifier for all merchandise you send to them so that , they will always know what inventory at the warehouse is yours. This unique identifier is part of the barcode that is printed on your label printer. Before you process your inventory, you need to create a *batch* and an *MSKU*.

Batch is the name you give a group of inventory. For example, if you just returned from the Arlington Public Library book sale, you might call your batch "Arlington Book Sale" so it is clear. Once you create a batch, you can continue to add items until you are ready to ship. If you logout for a while and come back, your batch will be waiting for you to start again.

In addition to the batches you create, FBAScout users will create batches as they scan that will be uploaded here as well. I don't currently have an example, but an FBAScout batch is typically the date and time the batch was sent to FBAPower.

MSKU (usually pronounced "skew" or "em-skew") stands for "merchant stock keeping unit" and is the numbering system you use for your items. It ties a product and condition together (like a "new" toy or a "used-good" book) for as long as you choose to send in that item. In my simple system, I change my MSKU every month. I started with item #1 on October 1 and, as you can see, I sent 320 items to Amazon that month. Not only does this create a unique identifier for Amazon, but it also allows me to track how long it takes an item to sell and when I first sold a particular item. For example, I have toys that I first shipped in

December 2010 and still sell. Every time I scan the toy, the original MSKU comes up and I send in the toy under that MSKU. If you have several copies of the same book, like a Harry Potter, but with different conditions, you will have a unique MSKU for each condition – "new," "like new," "very good," and so on.

Regardless of the name you choose to use for your MSKU, it must *end* with "_001" or whatever number you want to start with. FBAPower will automatically advance the number with each item you list. Each item MUST have a unique number.

1. Create a name for your batch. Select "new," type in your desired name and save it.
2. Type your MSKU into the box, ending with "_001."
3. Grab your first item and your scanner.
4. Place your cursor in the screen box on FBAPower that says "UPC, ISBN."
5. Find the barcode and scan your item.
6. The number should appear in the box that says "UPC, ISBN."
7. A listing will appear on the page for that item.

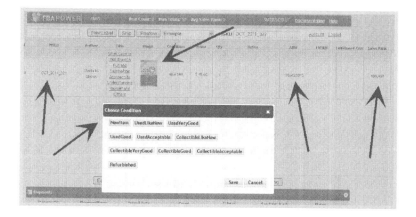

8. On the previous page you can see that the MSKU number is listed, then the information about the item. I'm going to choose "New Item." To the right is the ASIN (ASIN=Amazon Site ID Number), which is Amazon's unique page number for this item on its site. If you ever have trouble finding the ISBN# or UPC code for an item but can find it on the Amazon site, copy the ASIN# from the Amazon page for that book or product and paste it into the ISBN box in FBAPower and it will work just as well. "Sales rank" tells me that this book has sold copies recently.

9. After you choose a condition, you will automatically go to the "Price" screen.

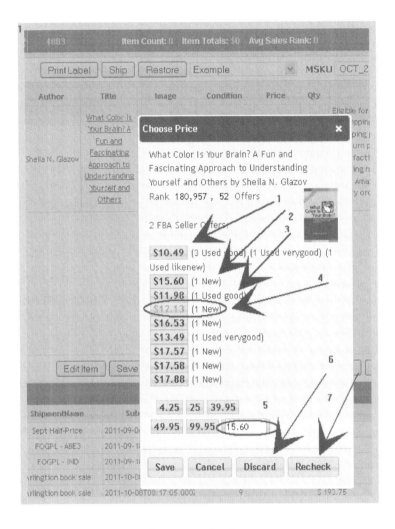

10. There's a lot to notice here:

1) It will be difficult to tell in a black
& white book, but the $10.49 is
red. Red is the color for merchant
sellers of used products. This

shows you that there are 5 offers by merchant sellers and all of them are for $10.49 ($6.50 + $3.99 shipping and handling). FBAPower automatically adds the $3.99 shipping into the offer price so you know the minimum for your pricing.

2) The next box is purple. Purple is a merchant seller with a new item. You will see that FBAPower priced my book at $15.60 to match the merchant seller's price + shipping and handling.

3) The next item is green. Green is another FBA Seller. As you can see, this seller has a copy of the book in "good" condition that he is selling for $11.98.

4) Ka-boom! This item is yellow, which indicates Amazon's price. Amazon always sells new. Amazon is selling this book new for $12.13. Why is everyone else selling their books so high if Amazon's price is $12.13? That's a good question. It is crazy to price higher than Amazon *unless*

Amazon is out of stock, of course. That may be the case here. Another possibility is that Amazon lowered its price recently and the other sellers haven't caught on yet. Lastly, it could just be poor pricing by the other sellers. Regardless, _you_ are not going to make the mistake of pricing higher than Amazon.

5) This is the price that FBAPower auto-filled for me. I'm going to change it to $10.75. I need to be lower than Amazon by at least $1 or else there's really no incentive to buy from me versus Amazon.

6) If for some reason I didn't like what I saw and decided not to send the item to Amazon, the "Discard" button would erase the item from my screen.

7) "Re-check" is primarily used if you come back to an item later and you want to make sure the pricing is still the same. I use it mostly for toys that I send in regularly. FBAPower will fill in the information from before. I click

"Re-check" on the pricing to see if I need to adjust.

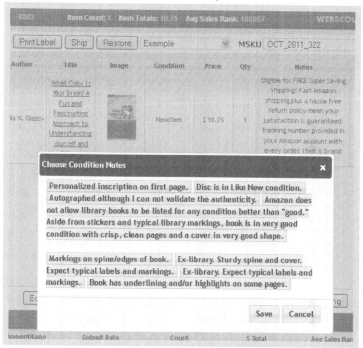

8) Next, you can choose condition notes. Click anywhere on the "notes" section for this item and this screen will pop up. Here you can see some of my customized notes. For "New Item," I don't normally click on condition notes because "new" speaks for itself, but now you know what it looks like. If I wanted to choose one of these notes, I would click on it and it would

automatically appear at the end of my "Notes" for this item.

9) If you want to write something specific that is not covered in your notes, click on the "Edit" button near the bottom of the listings page, and write it in. In addition, if you have multiple copies of an item, you'll need to click "Edit" and change the number from "1" to however many you have.

10) Now, click "print label" at the top left of the page. The first time you do this in each session, another tab will open and you'll be switched over to that tab. For the next listing, you will stay on the listing page. If there are any adjustments you still need to make to your printer, now is the time. Otherwise, click "print." If you have multiples of the same item, you can select the number of label copies to print.

11) Put labels on your items. Cover the ISBN or UPC code with your label.

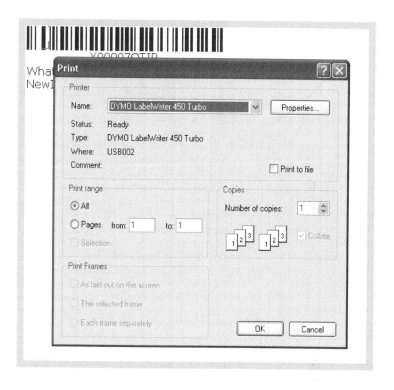

12) **When you click "OK" to print the label, it will not only print the label but also fill in the rest of the blanks on your listing.**

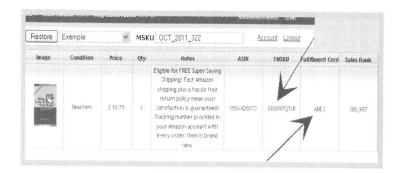

13) The FNSKU is a unique combination of letters and numbers that is printed on your label along with a barcode. It identifies this item as belonging to you, the condition and, basically, every piece of information about this item. When it is scanned at the warehouse, your listing will immediately go "live" on Amazon. You don't have to do anything with this – just make sure that the label goes on the right product.

14) Under "Fulfillment Center" you see "ABE3." This is one of Amazon's many warehouses. This particular one is in Pennsylvania outside of Philadelphia. It is right across the street from "ABE2." Other warehouses are in Indiana, Phoenix, Texas, Tennessee and elsewhere.

15) Take a felt-tip or permanent marker pen and mark the warehouse for your item on the box flap somewhere. This will help you keep your merchandise sorted properly should you end up needing to send your items to more than one warehouse. I have had batches where I ended up sending merchandise to five different warehouses.

16) Every time you print a label, your item is saved.

17) If you don't have a label printer yet and are planning to use Amazon's sheet-fed labels, then click on the "FNSKU" space instead of "Print." Your item will automatically be saved, a FNSKU number will be generated and the warehouse code will appear.

18) <u>This is very important!</u> Any item not saved will be discarded (i.e. deleted) the next time you log out OR time out.

19) Place the label over the barcode/ISBN # on your item. The folks who scan in Amazon's warehouse do not want to accidentally scan the wrong code.

20) Place the item in your box – preferably with the label facing up for faster scanning in the warehouse.

21) Next, list the rest of your items. If you have items going to a different warehouse, be sure to create and label a separate box for them.

22) As you go along, you may notice some numbers at the top of your screen:

23) "Item count" is the number of items in your order. "Item Totals" tells you how much you've priced this batch so far. If you knew, for example, that you had spent about $300 at the Arlington book sale, this number should make you very happy. "Avg Sales Rank" tells you your average sales rank. Because my shipments tend to be mixed media, this number is not particularly helpful to me. Still, low is good. I would be less-than-happy if this number was over 1 million, for example.

Pack and ship your box to Amazon

Now you have at least one box ready to go to Amazon, right? The next step is to pack it up according to Amazon's requirements. If you've read your contract, you already know that you cannot use foam peanuts in your shipment. To fill in gaps in your box and to secure your items, you may use bubble wrap and air pillows as well as clean white paper or clean newsprint (i.e. no ink on it – you can buy it in big rolls). The better and tighter you pack, the less filler you will need.

Leave the box flaps open for now. Weigh your box and write the weight on the flap near the warehouse information – "ABE3 – 48 lbs." Remember that your box cannot weigh more than 50 pounds. In addition, you need to round up. So if your box is 48 pounds and 8 ounces, for example, round up to 49 pounds.

Back at your FBAPower screen, click on the "Ship" button.

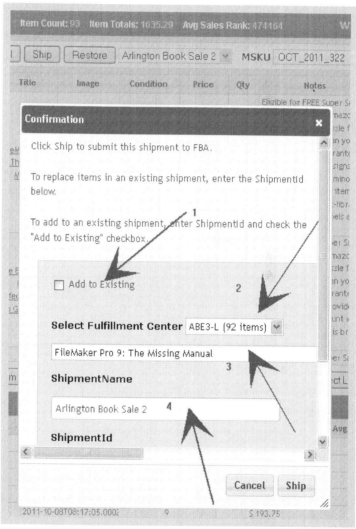

1. "Add to Existing" is used if you have additional items you want to add to a shipment you've already created and "shipped" to the Amazon website. In the future, if you select this button, you will need to change the Shipment Name and Shipment ID to match the one to which you have additions. For now, ignore it.

2. "Select Fulfillment Center" shows you the warehouse to which your items will go.

3. Right below it is a drop box where you can look at everything that is going to ABE3-L. If you have items going to multiple warehouses, you will need to click "Ship" as many times as there are warehouses until the main screen is empty.

4. "Shipment Name" is generally not changed, but you can if you want to.

5. The "Shipment ID" is not changed, either, unless you are trying to add new items to a shipment already in queue at Amazon. Otherwise, leave it alone and press "Ship".

6. Repeat these steps until all your items have been shipped. Your FBAPower screen should now be empty.

7. Log out and go to your Amazon seller account at: https://sellercentral.amazon.com and log in.

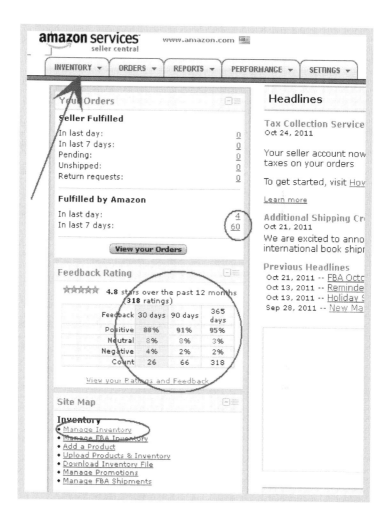

8. **Don't be afraid! This page only looks overwhelming at first. Right now, you are interested in going to the "Manage Inventory" screen. There are two ways you can do that: 1) the tab at the top of the page**

or 2) the link under "Site Map" at the bottom.

9. There's a lot of other information on this page that you'll want to look at later. I circled the feedback because you'll want to check it regularly. I have three recent customers who gave me a neutral on the same day (which Amazon counts as "negative") or negative feedback. I've gone back to them to try to resolve their issues, and to get them to remove the negative ratings. I've had customers give me a negative review because they didn't like the content of a book – as if I had anything to do with that! Anyway, most folks will remove negative feedback if you are responsive, polite and cheerful with them.

10. Now that you are in "manage inventory," you will see the inventory you've sent to Amazon. On the left you can see your inventory as either "Active" or "Inactive." Inactive means you've sold it and archived it because you are not selling it anymore. Active means it is for sale on Amazon's site.

11. The link "Inventory Amazon Fulfills" is more relevant for people who are both merchant sellers and FBA sellers. In your case, your "all inventory" and "Amazon fulfills" pages will

have the same items. From the screen on the next page (see the arrow on the left), you can also search for an item by its title, SKU, ISBN or ASIN number.

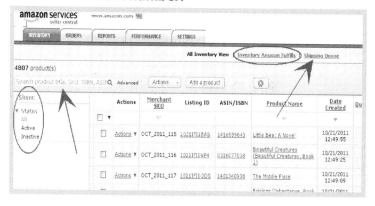

12. Click on the link that says "Shipping Queue."

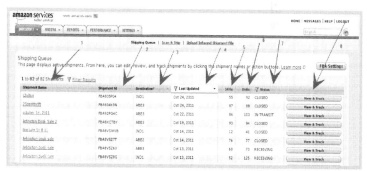

13. This page has a lot of important information for you:

1) This is your shipment name that you gave in FBAPower during the "ship" process.

2) This is the Shipment ID. You'll need this number and the Shipment name if you want to add something to a shipment after it has been sent to queue (but *before* it has actually been shipped to Amazon).

3) This is the warehouse destination; as you can see, there are a lot of them.

4) "Last updated" will also reflect the last time either you or Amazon did something with the shipment. As you can see here "Chilton" was updated on Oct 24, 2011 when Amazon finished scanning the order into their warehouse.

5) SKUs are the unique identifiers you have in the shipment.

6) Units are the actual number of units. If you have multiples of one or more items, then there will be more units than SKUs.

7) Status is fairly meaningless because Amazon is so bad about updating it. As you can see, I have shipments that say "In-Transit" or "Receiving" that are closed. Amazon sends you emails when your inventory reaches the warehouse, which is much more helpful to me.

8) Mine all say "View & Track" because I don't have a new shipment to process right now.

Yours will be different because you still have to process your order. Click on it now.

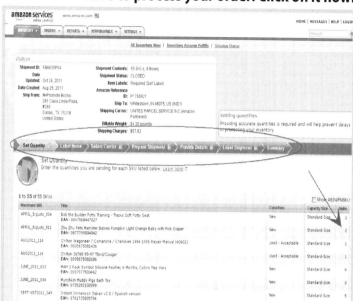

14. As you can see here, Amazon has a six-step process to preparing your boxes. This page is to set quantity.

15. You should already have your quantities filled in here for you by FBAPower. However, if you made a mistake and need to add or subtract a unit after the batch has been sent to Amazon's Shipping Queue, this is the place to do it.

16. Assuming everything is OK, press "Continue" at the bottom of this page to go to the next step, "Label Items."

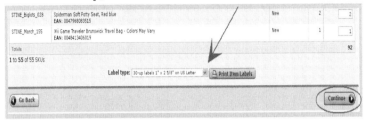

17. <u>If you don't have a label printer</u>, this is where you will be able to print sheet labels (30 on a page). Choose your labels and click on "Print Item Labels."

18. Place the labels on your items carefully, covering the barcode and/or ISBN#.

19. Place the items in your boxes with the labels facing up (if possible) for faster scanning in the warehouse.

20. Click "Continue" when you are done.

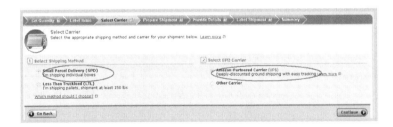

21. Click on "Small Parcel Delivery" and "Amazon-Partnered Carrier" and then "Continue." Amazon's carrier is UPS.

22. For the next step, you need to put in the number of boxes under "packing slips" and press the "print" button.

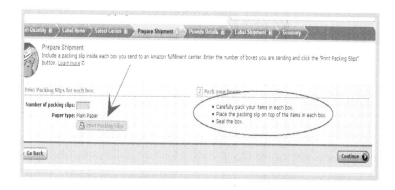

23. Make sure each box has a packing slip sitting on the top of the packed items.

24. Write down the weights of each box on a piece of paper if they are not readily visible. This is why I write the weight on the flap next to the warehouse. It saves a step later.

25. Seal the boxes.

26. On the next page, you'll type in the weights and dimensions of each box. If the box is a standard size (18"x12"x12" or smaller), you don't need to put in dimensions. If it is

bigger, however, you will be charged more and need to record it.

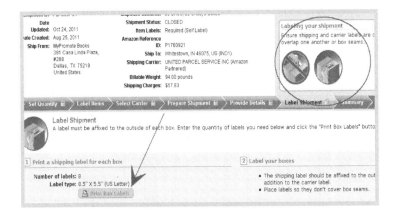

27. **Amazon fills in the number of box labels you need. If you don't have your free labels from UPS yet, you can print on paper and tape the paper to the box.**

28. **Make sure your labels don't overlap a box seam.**

29. **Click "Continue."**

30. **There's just one last thing to do! On the Summary page, you'll want to change the "Shipment Status" to "Shipped." Mine says "Closed" in this picture because it is old. By marking a shipment "Shipped," Amazon knows it is coming.**

31. Now take your boxes to a UPS drop-off
location or arrange for UPS to pick up from
your location and you are done! Pat yourself
on the back!

TAKE ACTION!

- Set up your USB scanner

- Set up your label printer (if you have one)

- Make sure your settings in FBAPower read the
way you want

- Determine your own SKU and Batch naming
system

- List, label and ship your first box(es) to Amazon

- Note how long it takes them to get to the
warehouse(s)

Cynthia Stine ·

12

SHOPPING WITH FBASCOUT!

Are you ready to go a little nuts? Shopping is the best part of the business. There's nothing quite like finding a super bargain. I've been known to squeal, gasp and jump up and down, depending on who is around me. Some deals are so good, I have to scan them several times to convince myself that they are real. This is the fun part of the business!

My friend Lesley found a super thrift store and we go together when we can for the sheer joy of it. Sometimes it is hard not to run laps around the store when we find a book or DVD for 10 cents and it registers as $30 or $40 on Amazon.

My dad recently found a discontinued item at Toys "R" Us for $3 that he's selling like crazy on Amazon for $65. Yep. $65. Our stores are completely sold out in North Texas.

At a book sale recently, I was buying books for 30 cents in "very good" and "like new" condition which I'll sell for $7 to $45. Rumplestiltskin has nothing on an FBA seller when it comes to turning straw into gold!

In this chapter, I'll briefly go over setting up your FBAScout and Scanfob scanner and then show you how to use FBAScout while shopping.

Set up your smartphone

It is not required to have a Scanfob 2002 to make FBAScout work. You can enter ISBN#'s manually, use the phone's built-in camera to take a picture of the ISBN# or use the voice-activated function on your phone (most Androids have this – not sure about the iPhone). A free application called "Zebra Xing" can be accessed from FBAScout and reads barcodes with the phone's camera. Regardless of whether you have a wireless scanner, you'll occasionally need to enter numbers manually or by voice simply because some items don't have barcodes.

I love having the Scanfob because it makes shopping fast and I have limited time, but it was my biggest hardware expense. If you go to http://fbascout.com/bluetooth-scanners/ and scroll down, you can get a discount on the Scanfob through FBAScout. Normally $349, you can get it for $282.

You need a smartphone in order to use the FBAScout application. This can be an iPhone, an iPad, an iPod touch or a phone with the Android operating system. The phone must have at least 3G. If you have an unlimited data plan, that's good – just make sure you have a reasonable data plan. AT&T allows 2MG per month, which is more than enough.

Next, download the FBAScout application to your phone. You can find it either on iTunes (for iPhone users) or at the Android Market™. Surf out to your app site from the phone and click "download" to install it. You get 250 free scans before you need to register and pay.

To   register,   watch   this   video: http://bit.ly/fbascoutvideo. Basically, you need to go to "settings" for FBAScout and put in your FBAPower email and password.

If you've got the Scanfob 2002, then watch the videos   on downloading the SerialMagic™ Gears application   you   need   to   make   it   work (http://bit.ly/installSerialMagic Gears) and pairing your Bluetooth   with   the   phone (http://bit.ly/fbascoutpairing).

A word about Scanfob

One of the most frequent calls I've gotten from my friends and family is about pairing the Bluetooth Scanfob scanner to their phone. They are usually standing in a store wondering why it is not working. So, before you head out the first time, be sure you've been able to make the Scanfob work at home first! Every time you want to shop, you need to make sure that the Scanfob is connected to the phone:

1. Turn on the Scanfob by holding down the tiny button on top until the blue light flashes.
2. Go into the SerialMagic Gears program and click the "Connect" button – it may also say "Re-connect." Assuming it connects...
3. Open FBAScout.
4. Scan a barcode.

If it doesn't connect or gets hung up on connecting (give it about 10 seconds or so), you may need to re-boot your phone and start over. If it is still having trouble connecting:

- Go into the Bluetooth settings on your phone and click the button that says "make device discoverable" or "make device findable."
- Click on the Scanfob you see at the bottom of the settings page and *unpair* it.
- Pair it again. You will need to put in the "0000" code into your phone again.
- Your blue light should be flashing on the Scanfob as you pair it again.
- Go back to SerialMagic Gears and try "Connect" again. It should work.

- Switch over to FBAScout and test a barcode.

If nothing else works, go to www.serialio.com/contact.php and they will help you set up your Scanfob and SerialMagic Gears program.

<u>Shopping</u>

Now you are ready to shop. When you arrive at the store, assemble your Scanfob and phone. If you are interested in a slick assembly, look at Chris Green's Borg-like solution [http://bit.ly/1handscout]. That is a "number 1," not an "el" in the URL. He has links at the bottom of the page to the parts you need. You will be assimilated! (Non-trekkers roll your eyes here.)

1. Press the top of your Scanfob (the tiny black square) until the blue light begins to flash.
2. Open SerialMagic Gears on your phone.
3. Click on "connect."
4. Once the scanner is connected to the phone, open the FBAScout application.
5. If you are using an armband/wristband to carry your phone hands-free, slide it carefully into the case.
6. Start scanning!

FBAScout gives you strategic information:

- Weight (makes a difference for textbooks and really heavy items)
- Rank
- Amazon's price (if Amazon is selling the item)
- Department (Books, Toys, Electronics, etc.)
- New offers from Merchant sellers
- Used offers from Merchant sellers
- FBA Sellers
- How many of the item each seller has in stock
- Your net price as an FBA seller

I've sold a lot of these and for a long time I was the *only* seller, not just the only FBA seller. You can see it weighs 4.2 pounds, which means I have to allow for higher shipping costs. Plus, what you can't tell from the picture is it requires an oversize box. Still, my margin is good and I sell at least one a day when I have them in stock so it is well worth it to me. I've learned that a rank like this equals at least a sale a day in Baby.

Next to each seller's offering price, you see a number in parentheses. That number is how many of the item that seller has for sale. Below each FBA seller's offering price, you see another dollar figure. That number represents the seller's net. The net is calculated for you by FBAScout. It represents what Amazon will send you after commissions and fees are subtracted. You can then subtract your acquisition cost from that number to get a close idea of how much you'll actually make from this item. This number does NOT include your shipping costs to Amazon. If there is no FBA seller, there will be no net calculation.

This is a tremendous tool for you as a seller and one that no other scanner on the market offers. For example, what if the $44.99 seller had 200 units? Would that affect my decision to buy? You bet it would! Now I can see that I would have to price my items lower than the other guy – and to keep lowering it if he keeps lowering it. Because I already know that I sell one-to-two units a day of this product when I am the *only* seller, a person with 200 units would have at least a six-month supply. I wouldn't want to have to wait until she/he sold out.

As it is, I'm the $45 seller and I don't mind waiting a few days. With this particular item, my margin is less than the 3X I like to get. It sells so fast, however, that I don't mind and my profit is still around $20 an item.

Here I'm trying to sell my used scanner that I bought to use with my ASellerTool PDA. While the numbers initially look exciting, I'm wary. There is no rank to tell me if this item has actually sold for these prices. I looked up the scanner on eBay and on the manufacturer's website and I found out this scanner is two generations behind what is currently available. Plus, you can buy it on eBay for about $100. If I decide to sell mine on Amazon, I will price it for a lot less than these prices.

This is why the consumer electronics ("CE") department is so tricky. There are over 1.5 million items in this department and if you don't know what you're looking at, you could buy something that will take months to years to sell. If you see a deal on consumer electronics in a Big Lots flyer, you might want to check it out online before you go to the store.

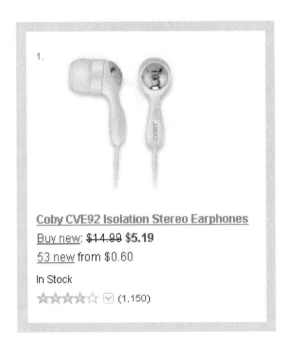

1.

Coby CVE92 Isolation Stereo Earphones
Buy new: $14.99 $5.19
53 new from $0.60
In Stock
★★★★☆ ✓ (1,150)

As of this writing, this is the most popular item in consumer electronics. I know this because Amazon lets you sort its departments by "most popular" (a great way to do research on trends, by the way). Here is the information Amazon has on the product:

> Product Dimensions: 8.6 x 4 x 1.2 inches ; 2.4 ounces
> Shipping Weight: 1 pounds (View shipping rates and policies)
> Shipping: This item is also available for shipping to select countries outside the U.S.
> ASIN: B000FOYMKU
> Item model number: cve92
> Average Customer Review: 3.8 out of 5 stars See all reviews (1,150 customer reviews)
> Amazon Best Sellers Rank:
>
> - #2 in Electronics > Accessories & Supplies > Audio & Video Accessories > Headphones
> - #9 in Electronics > Portable Audio & Video > MP3 Players & Accessories > MP3 Player Accessories
> - #9 in Electronics > Portable Audio & Video > Accessories
>
> Date first available at Amazon.com: July 7, 2004

So even though Amazon doesn't always give a rank in CE like it does for other categories, from this information you can tell this would be a good item to buy for resale on Amazon – if the margins are right, which they probably aren't unless you can get the headsets for 25 cents.

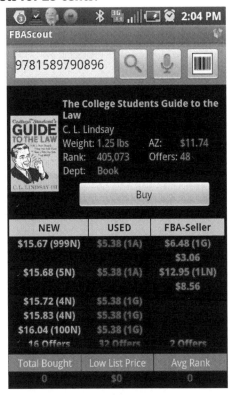

Of course, "Books" is the department in which most people sell. There are over 10.5 million *ranked* books in Amazon's catalog and the number grows daily at a rate of over 200,000 per year. There are 33.6 million books listed on Amazon, which means that 23.1 million books have not sold a single unit and have no rank. This guide to the law is a fun-looking book that I bought for $1 at a book sale. My copy is a library edition so I can only sell it for "good."

I see the rank is 405,073 which tells me Amazon has sold this book fairly recently and it is in my personal rank criteria.

What price do you think I might give my book? I'll probably price it around $7. Do you see why? Nearly every seller of this book is selling it above Amazon's current price of $11.74 – madness! One poor merchant seller (probably the author) has nearly 1000 copies priced at $15.67! It is possible that Amazon has recently dropped its price and the other sellers haven't caught up yet. Regardless, I have to price my used library edition to compete with Amazon's brand-new copy at $11.74.

I am pricing my book higher than the one priced at $6.48, even though the condition is the same, because there is a decent chance that book will sell before my book gets to the warehouse. It takes about a week from where I live in Texas for a shipment of books to get to Pennsylvania and be processed by the warehouse team. For this reason, I often disregard the lowest prices set by competitors if I think the book is selling several copies a month.

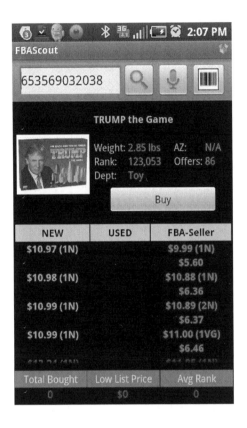

    I found this game still factory-sealed at a book sale for $1. Do you see that copy up there for $11 in "VG" condition? That seller is "Amazon Warehouse Deals." They are the only ones who can sell a toy or game used. If you were to send up a game in "Used" condition, it would languish in the warehouse until you fixed the error. FBA sellers can only sell toys new or as "Collectible." In addition, you can only sell a game as "Collectible" if it is discontinued. There are "Collectible-

Very Good" sellers of this game (not visible on the screenshot) and they are taking a risk of losing their selling privileges on Amazon. It hardly seems worth the risk for a $25 game. But *you* won't make that mistake. I will probably price my "New" game at $10.89 or $11.00. At a ranking of 123,053, Amazon is selling several games a month, BUT we are about to hit the holiday buying season where it will sell more copies.

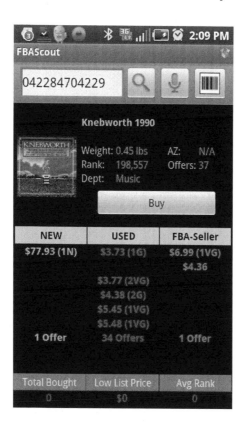

Remember what I said earlier about blindly following other people without knowing why they bought something? Under normal circumstances, I might not have bought this CD because the rank is so high. Mine is in "Good" condition (the discs are excellent but the jewel box is scuffed up). I got it for 10 cents because *I* wanted it for myself. After I copy the files to my computer, I'll sell it and I don't care that it might take a very long time to sell. If I price it at $6, I'll make around $3.50, which is great. But I would probably send it in even if I only made 50 cents because I bought it first for personal use and, because the item is so lightweight and small, storage will be 2 or 3 cents a month.

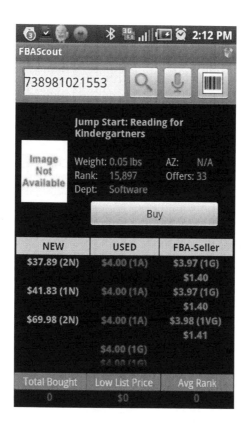

I've learned that this is an OK rank in software. I sold a piece of software ranked around 16,000 that took three months to sell. Because I acquired this game/educational software for 10 cents, I'm fine with making $1.30. I'll price this at $3.97. Notice, I'm not pricing it at $3.95. I don't want to trigger a price war. A lot of the repricing software will just keep dropping prices if someone else does. By keeping the same price, no price war. Now that I'm not competing on price, I can compete on other factors like my description, my feedback stats and how long I've been selling on Amazon. When all offers are equal, buyers look for other distinguishers. Or, I could just get lucky and be first on the list. Regardless, my product will eventually sell and I've turned 10 cents into $1.30, which is the equivalent of $1 into $13 if I do it 10 times – straw into gold!

Now that we've had some fun shopping, let's look at some of the other features of FBAScout that make my life easier. First, the "Buy" button. If you decide to buy an item while scouting, click on "Buy" and put in how many you are buying. You can also put in the price you paid for it. FBAPower is working on a feature where the price you paid will appear with the item in its other programs FBAPower and FBARepricer. Today, I grab my old receipts (sorted by month) to determine if I have enough margin to lower my prices. In the future, it will be embedded in FBARepricer if I include it at the time I buy or list my product. If you capture the price now, it will show up later when those features are ready.

Then you can go back to scanning. If you want to add quantities or delete an item from your list, use the "Switch view" button, which you get when you press the menu button at the bottom left of your phone.

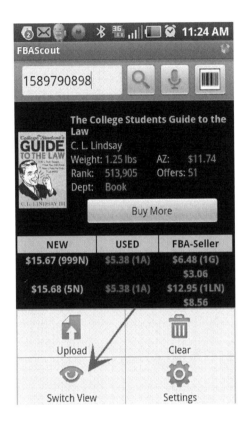

In the next picture, you can see that I've bought one item so far. If I want to change my item, I just click on it.

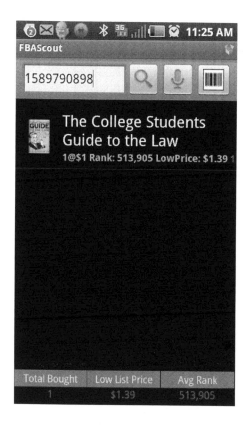

Just click "Switch View" in the menu bar again to go back. The other thing to do from the menu screen is to "Upload." While you are standing in line at the checkout register, click on Upload to send your entire list to FBAPower. You can pull down your batch later under "Batch" in FBAPower, where it will say "FBAScout" and the date so you know which one to pull up. You will still need to add condition and price, and print labels, but this will save you the time of scanning each item, which can easily add up — a typical book sale haul is over 100 items, for example.

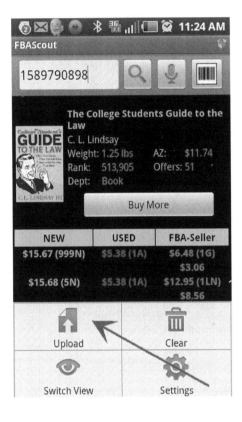

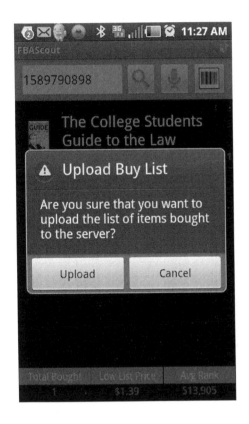

A few other features of FBAScout:

- The ISBN# screen is where your scanner will put the number. However, if you tap here, you can enter a number manually. This is very helpful for books without a barcode (generally books published before 1980).

- Another way to enter a number is by voice command. Click on the microphone to speak the number into FBAScout. You need to say the numbers smoothly with no significant pauses.

* If you click on the barcode symbol at the top, your phone's camera will activate. Hold your phone over the barcode and let the auto-focus feature of your phone zoom in on the barcode. Once it reads the barcode, the number will appear in the ISBN# screen, as will the data pulled from Amazon. This is a very handy feature if you happen to be out and don't have your scanner with you. You wouldn't want to attend a book sale and scan this way, but it is great for a few items.

TAKE ACTION!

* Set up your Scanfob and smartphone
* Have your criteria firmly in mind. You may even want to write down your "buy triggers" on a piece of paper to take with you
* Determine your shopping budget
* Go shopping
* Upload your items to FBAPower
* List, label and ship your items

Cynthia Stine

13

AMAZON'S IMPORTANT REPORTS FOR SELLERS!

By this point, your first shipment is on its way to the Amazon warehouse and you are probably wondering, "What's next?" The next thing to do is to familiarize yourself with Seller Central.

When your shipment reaches the warehouse, you will get a couple of emails from Amazon. The first will tell you it is in the warehouse. The second will tell you when your shipment has been processed and your listings are live.

That's when the fun begins. Assuming you had fast-selling items, you should see sales within the first week. I had my first sale within a few hours of my listings going live.

Now that you have sales, all those wonderful reports Amazon provides become relevant. The most important one is about the money, of course!:

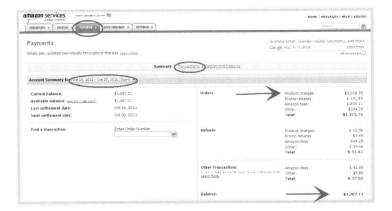

This page is the "Payments" report, which you'll find under "Reports" in the main navigational bar at the top of the page. As you can see, this covers the current two-week payment period. You can access previous payments under the drop down menu circled in the picture.

This is a summary page. You can click on "Transactions" to see all the transactions that make up this report. This is particularly helpful as you are coming up to speed on Amazon's fees. I broke out those fees earlier in this book, but they are hard to understand until you see them in action here on your Payments report. Transactions include *everything* from shipping via UPS to refunds (it happens to everyone) to commissions. All you need to do is subtract your inventory acquisition and shipping supply expenses from this number.

Selling on Amazon is a bit like buying and selling real estate. Your money is made at the time of the deal. Don't take a bad deal and hope it will get better later. If you make wise choices with your purchases and build in cushion for price fluctuations, refunds and other expenses, you'll do well.

By the way, the "Refunds" on this page are not necessarily buyer refunds. Amazon uses this section to charge and then refund you money for Prime buyers using expedited shipping. It is to your benefit, but the accounting can be confusing when you look at it the first time.

As you sell inventory, be sure to run the other reports Amazon gives you and learn how they can help you. Most of them are Excel files that you download to your computer.

The other pages where you will spend a lot of time are your Inventory pages.

On this page you can see how many SKUs you have used with Amazon. I don't actually have over 4000 items currently in inventory – that is simply how many SKUs I've sent to Amazon in the last year or so. You can switch the view on this page to only see "active" or only see "inactive" SKUs. You can sort the information on this page by the hyperlinked categories at the top of the chart – Merchant SKU, Product Name, Date Created and Price.

On this page, you can change your prices manually and they will take effect immediately. You can also search your inventory by title, SKU, ISBN and ASIN. The "Low Price" indicator is not particularly helpful to me since I am rarely the lowest-priced seller: still, when I am, it shows that with a green checkmark.

Now let's go to the "Inventory Amazon Fulfills."

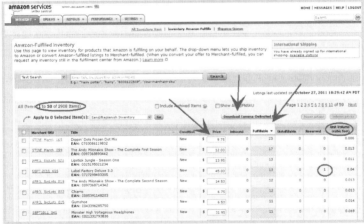

On this page, you notice that I have only 2908 SKUs. These are the ones that are currently active. I have greater search capabilities on this page. I can also search for items and perform bulk activities like "Send/Replenish Inventory" and others. I can download this report as a comma-delimited file, which opens in Excel, where, I can perform more strategic data sorts.

I can also change prices on this page manually. I've sorted this page by "Fulfillable" which shows me the items where I have the most units. I check these pretty regularly. Right now the prices on the "Andy Milonakis Show" DVDs have dropped to ridiculous levels and I'm waiting for some low-ball sellers to run out so I can clear the rest of my inventory. I only paid $3 a DVD, but there's no reason to take a loss if I don't have to. Same with the "Lipstick Jungle."

The Label Factory Deluxe 3.0 is doing very well for me. I bought them, in pristine condition, for $5 each at a clearance sale, and I smile every time one sells. The "Reserved" on the side means one has just sold, but not shipped. Buyers have a window of time to change their mind and that's why there's a "Reserved," which will be off this chart by the end of the day.

If you click the "Show ASIN/FNSKU" box at the top of the page, the listings will show you the ASIN number. You can click on that to see the product on that page and check prices. If you decide you want to change your price, come back to this page, change the price and then click "Submit Prices" at the top of the page. You can change as many prices as you like on this page before clicking "Submit Prices," but be sure to do it before going to the next page or your changes will not be saved.

Next, the "Unit Volume" in the last column shows you the measurements Amazon uses to calculate your storage fees. If you are ever curious as to which items are taking up the most amount of space, click here.

Lastly, there is one more important piece of information: how to get help. Amazon has wonderful seller support. You can get a live person on the phone and he or she will work with you until the problem is resolved. The Help link is at the top of every page.

In the middle of the Help page on the right-hand side is a button for you to contact Seller Support. I've noted with the arrows some links that you might find helpful, including the "Getting Started Guide" and "Webinar Schedule." Both of these have been helpful to me.

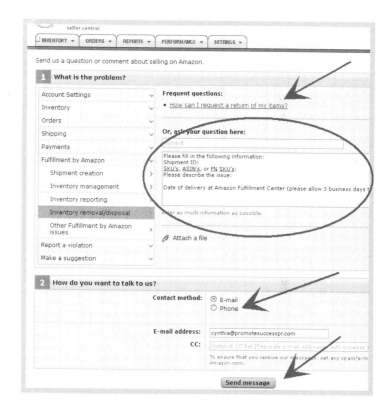

Amazon helps you define the problem. At the top, it offers a possible answer. If you need more help, fill in this form. Even if you plan to call them, fill in the information before you call because they will ask you for it. Then, you can choose either "E-mail" or "Phone." If you choose phone, type in a phone number and they will call you immediately or at a time of your choosing. They are also responsive to email.

Also, if you need help with FBAPower or FBAScout, you can contact that company at: info@fbapower.com, www.fbapower.com, or www.fbascout.com. In addition, the FBA Forum on Yahoo is a gold mine of information for FBA sellers, by FBA sellers. Just by searching past posts, you will likely find the answers to your questions. The FBAPower guys are on the forum, too: http://bit.ly/fbaforum.

TAKE ACTION!

- Become familiar with the reports Amazon gives you
- Check your inventory and payment reports frequently
- Sort your sales each month so you know which ones are subject to sales tax. Print off the list for each month for your records
- Learn the simple way to reprice through the "Inventory Amazon Fulfills" page

14

THEY DID IT!

As I mentioned in the beginning, I wrote this book because people kept asking me what I was doing and the PowerPoint presentation I created wasn't enough. Five people started Amazon FBA businesses over the past year and all of them have realized success. I am grateful to them for sharing their experiences and triumphs. I have learned so much from them in the process. Here are some of the lessons learned:

Discontinued Toy is Online Gold

My Dad has become an avid consumer of Big Lots and Toys"R"Us ads and coupons. He shops there regularly and gets good deals. One day he found a deal he couldn't believe was real when it popped up on his phone. He found a particular Xbox guitar controller that was selling "buy two, get one free" for $4.50 each.

For $9.00, he bought three and sent them in to Amazon priced at $65.00 each. They sold immediately. Then he ran out and bought as many more as he could find. Every time Toys"R"Us re-stocked, he bought them all.

He called me to tell me about it and I looked all over my local Toys"R"Us store. When I asked for help, I was told the product was discontinued and no longer for sale in their stores or online. Happily, for Dad, they were restocked several times in his store in Wilmington, North Carolina.

My Dad is a great example of someone for whom this business works part-time. He's the busiest retired guy you'll ever meet, with board meetings, tennis matches and church responsibilities. This business allows him to make extra income in his own time and way. He is able to take advantage of the two-hour and one-day sales that often occur in the middle of a week. Before starting this business, he knew nothing about toys. Now he knows what's important – people will pay for what they want and just because it doesn't make sense to him, doesn't mean he can't sell it.

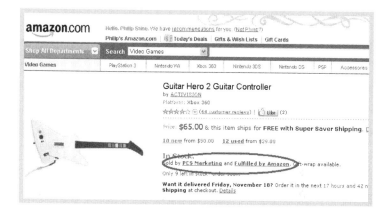

Choosy Moms Drive the Baby Market

On my first Big Lots shopping trip, Chris Green taught me a lot about the concept of "anything with a barcode." While toys made perfect sense to me, I hadn't thought about baby items (or many of the other categories for that matter). Chris found a particular brand of baby wipes for under $2 that were selling online for $25.

My eyes goggled. Twenty-five dollars for butt wipes? When diapers and wipes are sold in practically every store? As a parent of young kids himself, Chris spoke authoritatively when he said, "If your kid likes a particular brand of anything, you'll buy it." They did have a nice smell. Plus, they were probably discontinued according to Chris. He bought out the store's stock and sold them all online. A few months later I found some more and sold them, too. Since my happy experience with butt wipes, I've sold adult diapers, too.

As another example of how choosy (mostly) moms drive the baby market, a friend of mine in the business, John, found large quantities of a particular brand of pacifier that was discontinued. He was the only FBA seller. He couldn't believe the markup and hit every store within driving distance. At the peak of his pacifier sales, he was selling over 100 units a week. He's sold baby bottles, nipples (just talking about this with him made me giggle), spoons and baby toys. John doesn't even have children but he sells to choosy moms.

I've sold hundreds of baby spoons in the past year. I buy them for $3 or less at Big Lots and other stores and then I sell them for $10-$15 each. I love baby spoons. They are cheap, lightweight, sell fast and have a great margin. Who on earth would pay so much for a set of plastic spoons? My busy and impatient customers, that's who.

I have several designer diaper bags for sale along with my last remaining foam booster seat, a couple of mobiles, several different kinds of bathtub toys and baby puzzles. I expect all of them to sell by the end of December (2011).

Are You Willing to Get Dirty?

One of the best strategies for this business is to be where others are not. If everyone is sending in the latest gadget from Big Lots, you need to be somewhere else. I love Big Lots but sometimes the competition with other FBA sellers can be annoying – particularly when some of them participate in a "race to the bottom" that drives all the prices down.

My friend Lesley spotted a diamond in the rough at a thrift store in a more industrial part of town. When she walked in, the place was dirty, crowded, chaotic, loud and cluttered. Still, she gamely headed over to the bookshelves where she discovered that on Saturdays from 10 a.m. to 2 p.m., *all* the hardbacks were 20 cents and all the paperbacks were 10 cents.

For less than $10, she left with hundreds of dollars worth of books. She couldn't even go through them all in one session. When she came back again, she discovered that a lot of fresh (if dusty) inventory was on the shelves and she left again with hundreds of dollars worth of books for less than $10. When she took me, it went faster working as a team. We were able to look at video games (25 cents), videos (10 cents) and much, much more. We were completely filthy by the end of day and jubilant as we divvied up our finds. We go back there as often as we can.

Incompatible Business Models Can Be Complementary

I'm a big believer in "co-opetition" where you work together with selected competitors to help everyone succeed. Obviously you have to find the right partners, and it is important to understand what each person wants – it will not be the same for everyone, even though we all want to make money. Sometimes someone with an incompatible business model is a perfect fit.

Super-sleuth Lesley found a Craigslist ad where an Amazon merchant seller was offering his rejects for

$3 a box. When she checked out his warehouse, she learned that he had over 500,000 books for sale on Amazon on his shelves *and* thousands of boxes of new, like-new and very good books that didn't fit his profile. She took a few boxes to start and discovered that the merchant's team did not scan books without a barcode, which gave her some fantastic finds with older books. In addition, quite a few of the books that did not fit the merchant's model fit hers as an FBA seller. The ones that didn't work for her, she donated to her local library and charities. Most of them were blockbusters that will do very well with the reading public.

I went back with her on one trip and bought 65 boxes (all my garage could store at the time). Boy was I tired that day. I'm making my way through them in between more urgent shipments. I try to send boxes to Amazon regularly. Right now I'm focused on toys, games and gifts, but I'll get through those boxes as I generally clear around $120-$150 a box (on average). Not bad for a $3 investment.

Rethink Stores That Are Remodeling

I was annoyed when my local grocery store remodeled a few months ago. Nothing was in its regular place and the store was chaotic. It took twice as long to shop. What I didn't realize at first was how many non-food items are for sale at a grocery store. As part of its remodel, the store was clearing out its shelves at deeply discounted prices. I brought in my scanner and found all kinds of bargains both for my family and to sell online.

While we can sell food online FBA, I haven't yet. Much of the food that was on sale was getting close to its expiration date, which was fine for us to eat, but I wouldn't have wanted to send it to Amazon. I also found kitchen gadgets, toys, games and small appliances on sale that were fine for FBA.

On another day, I stepped inside an office supply store that was undergoing major renovations. They had a big banner up outside that said, "We're Open!" underneath the scaffolding. I came to buy some stickers and left with hundreds of dollars of computer games, software and manuals. The brand-new games were $1 each and I sold them for $12-$20. There were over 20 copies of the LabelFactory Deluxe software at $5 each and I'm selling them for $45 each. I bought an old version of Microsoft FrontPage for $25 and sold it within two weeks for $252.99.

Now I look for stores that are remodeling. I found another office supply store this morning that was remodeling. I bought 35 software packages for $5 each and eight iPad cases for $5 each. With one exception, all are selling at $20 and up. I'm expecting to clear around $600 after expenses and I spent about 20 minutes in the store – that's a good return on investment even when you add in the hour or so I'll spend removing price stickers, labeling and shipping to Amazon.

What Were They Thinking?

Some stores buy popular merchandise for all the wrong reasons. When a customer enters the door, they usually have a specific idea of what they want and why they think they'll find it at that particular retail outlet. If they find something outside of that expectation – even if it is something they might gladly buy in another environment – they leave it alone.

I went into a Blockbuster one day to rent a video and was surprised to see a big clearance table with vacuum cleaners, wall stickers, plush toys, books and an assortment of other bewilderments. They were at a deep discount and I bought most of them. The vacuum cleaners sold so fast, they hardly spent any time at all in the warehouse. I profited from that experience and now I keep an eye out for stores selling items that are weird for their category. There is a good chance that item will be on sale later.

Other stores stock up seasonally on merchandise, like toys and games that they don't sell year-round. They may offer discounts before, during and after the season. For this reason, I plan to keep an eye open at Home Depot, Lowes and my local grocery store right after Christmas for steep discounts. Toys sell all year on Amazon.

I bought Toy Story 3 games this year at Aldi's grocery in my neighborhood for $19.99 and listed them for $50. Another enterprising FBA seller has one listed for $79.99. I'm not sure about that price being able to stick. However, if he sells his one copy before mine get to the warehouse, then I'll raise my prices!

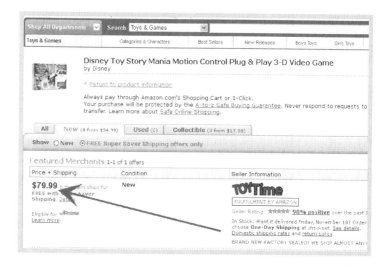

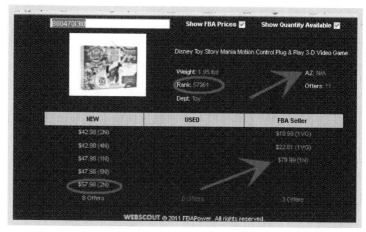

As you can see from this image, the toy is a good
seller, Amazon is not selling it and the only other new
FBA offer is $79.99. That seller only has one copy. I
priced mine at $50, which is more than most of the

merchant sellers although not the very highest. I may have to experiment with price until I get it just right.

This image is of WebScout, which comes free with FBAPower. I use WebScout when I'm repricing to tell me how many units my competitors have. It helps me decide whether I should lower my price or wait them out.

See those guys selling the toy used? They are actually "Collectible-Very Good" sellers. Webscout and FBAScout don't distinguish between "Used" and "Collectible" offers, but I checked them out when writing this book.

Just Do It!

My friend Lynn started her business a few weeks ago (November 2011) and is realizing incredible success with holiday sales (Dec 9, 2011) so far. She has great intuition for what will be popular and made some super toy buys (and sales!) before a lot of other FBA Sellers caught on to how hot they were. She taught me about Inkoos and together we bought out our local Targets in Dallas and Chicago. She proved to me that there were deals to be found at Target – I never seriously scouted there before she told me what she found – and Wal-Mart.

She immediately understood margin and that an "OK" deal was really a bad deal because it took money and attention away from the next really good deal. She quickly realized there were more deals than she could possibly buy and so she picks and chooses. She got a Target credit card while standing in the checkout line. She not only got bonus savings for signing up that day, she now saves 5% on all her purchases until she reaches her limit each month. As long as you pay off the card quickly, it is a great deal. If you carry a balance, the rate is around 22% - steep.

She follows the "3X" rule. As a busy mom and college student, she does not have time for any activity or purchase that isn't going to be productive. One of her personal rules is that she won't buy anything too big to fit in one of her box sizes (18"x12"x12" or 20"x20"x20") because it is too much time and hassle – even with a big payout. She would rather buy and sell three or four smaller items and get the same profit, than to have to find a special box size, call UPS to pick it up, etc., for an oversized item. This is her rule. Once I sold my first slow cooker for $71, I bought a bunch of bigger boxes. You will have your own rules.

Lynn test-drove this book and made it much better with her feedback. She got her business up and running in a week and she is selling more than I am in my second holiday season. She had me to answer her questions, which helped speed the process, but all the work was hers and she is reaping the rewards. Her second check from Amazon was over $7,500!

With my friend Lesley, I told her about FBA and before I even knew how interested she was, she had started her business – and her brother, too. She discovered the huge warehouse where we can buy books for $3 a box and the thrift store that sells books for 10 cents on Saturdays. Lesley is also the one that told me about an unbelievable one-day sale at Tuesday Morning one weekend. I'll make about $4K off the inventory I bought in a few hours. I learn as much from Lesley as she ever did from me about this business.

My friend John took about two-three weeks to get everything set up and he had trouble with the technology (he is also a Mac user so I could not help him), but once he was functioning, he is selling like crazy. He gives me great tips on baby items.

My dad took several months before he started sending in large shipments. He started with his books and media and he made small experiments. Now that he feels ready, he is like a house on fire. He calls me from Toys"R"Us or Big Lots with exciting finds and it tickles me. He was the first one to find the slow cookers at Big Lots and to encourage me to try a new category. Since then I've sold coffee makers, food processors and pressure cookers as well.

The common thread with all these stories is that they took the plunge and tried it. Each person's business is uniquely their own. The time they put into their businesses, the investment in inventory and the size of their businesses is a reflection of their personal values, resources and decisions – as yours will be – but they are all successful and happy that they started.

Cynthia Stine

15

YOU CAN DO IT, TOO!

You've come all this way and read the whole book. Hopefully, you are here because you have a shipment on its way to Amazon and thought you'd check in to see if I had anything else to say! I do, but not in this book.

If you've not yet taken action, now is the time. Make a commitment to yourself that you'll have at least one box on its way to Amazon by this time next week. The first sale – when you know for sure this business is going to work – is such a rush! And selling never gets old. I'm still thrilled every time I get an email telling me that something has sold.

It's a cliché, but if I can do it, you can too. I'm a wife and a mom trying to help my family make ends meet. What *is* remarkable about my story is that I can operate this business on such a small scale and be successful. It truly is a manageable part-time business. Now that you know how I do it, you can too. I have good tools to maximize my time and make me a smarter buyer, and I have a good partner in Amazon to help me reach the largest retail audience in the world and to meet their buying expectations.

This is not a risk-free business, but it is a risk-manageable business. The cost of entry is low and the rewards are high. I look forward to seeing you succeed online and would love to hear your fun stories of things that you can't believe sold, deals so good you felt guilty, and the joy of selling online overall.

Cheers,

MyPromote Books
www.fbastepbystep.com

16

DON'T MAKE MY MISTAKES!

Over the past year, I've made mistakes and learned a lot from them. You'll make mistakes, too, but hopefully you can make new mistakes instead of these!

1. Check the video/DVD/CD inside the case before you buy used media. Sometimes the case will not match the contents and you'll return home with junk instead of jewels.

2. Make sure the tape or disc is in good condition. Apply scratch filler if need be or don't buy it if you are not sure. Returns for poor product quality hurt your rating as a seller.

3. Don't sell a video, DVD or CD in "acceptable" condition. It is not worth creating an unhappy

customer. Books are OK in acceptable condition
– just be sure to let them know what they're
getting up front.

4. Beware of sets! I bought a bunch of Tae Bo
   videos not realizing that the prices I saw on the
   scanner were for the set, not individual tapes.
   This happens a lot with workout videos. Because
   I don't have a complete set – and have not been
   able to find the missing tape – the videos are
   gathering dust on my bookshelf.

5. Beware of different items with the same ISBN.
   This happens when there is an assortment or an
   item typically sells by the case. Pacifiers,
   diapers, medical supplies and items that sell in
   different colors should be checked more closely
   when you scan. I've learned to surf out to
   Amazon on my phone when something seems
   "too good to be true" or when the picture for a
   pink item and a blue item come up with the
   same image.

6. Don't price the same or higher than Amazon!
   More than once I've gotten home and
   discovered that I was so excited by the other FBA
   prices (nice and high) that I didn't see that
   Amazon was selling the product new for less. I

once returned 20 videos to Big Lots because I didn't notice this.

7. Don't sell calendars in January! You can sell calendars year round (I sold a 2011 calendar in September of the same year), but after the first week in January – watch out! That's when Amazon slashes all its calendar prices to the bone. In January, I had about 30 calendars left in inventory. Some that Amazon was selling below my cost, I decided to leave up there and see what happened. Others I dropped in price and cleared out. I've been surprised, but I've continued to sell a calendar or two every month and I only have five left in inventory. This year I plan to sell out by January.

8. Save your item listing! In FBAPower, you have to process or "save" every item in a batch or you'll lose it and need to re-scan it. When you print a label, the item is automatically saved. The problem comes up in the situation where you use FBAScout and upload items to your FBAPower. If you open the batch, but don't have time to process all the items, only the ones you processed are saved. Either don't open a batch until you are ready to process it, or quickly click through each non-processed item on the

"FNSKU" box. This will save the item and you can come back later.

9. Print off, read and re-read your contract with Amazon! It is horribly long but it includes very important issues to which you've agreed. For example, you cannot sell "advanced reader's copy" or "promotional use only" items in books and media. I sent in a bunch (I'm in the publishing business and had a ton in my personal library) and got a warning from Amazon. I ended up having Amazon destroy them for me. They are quite serious about this issue. Another example is that library books – no matter how nice – cannot list for better than "good" condition and you have to disclose that it is a library book.

10. Amazon is also very particular about how you ship boxes to them. No foam peanuts, no newspaper. Check all the fine print or be unpleasantly surprised later. Also, all items that have plush or cloth exposed must be covered in a plastic bag or shrink-wrapped so they don't get dirty in the warehouse. If you use bags, be sure to create safety warning labels and put one on each bag:

> WARNING! Keep away from small children. The thin film may cling to nose and mouth and prevent breathing.

11. Keep an eye on your inventory and pricing. Amazon lowers its prices without warning. Sometimes it is a short one-day (all mysteries 15% off!) or one-week sale, sometimes it is just a price cut to compete with its FBA sellers and/or clear out overstocked inventory. If you have many units of the item in question, be sure to check it manually and don't rely solely on your repricer. If it is an Amazon sale and not a permanent price cut, you may want to wait for the price to go back up.

12. Review your sales every day. I just about ripped my hair out when I realized that I had made a typo – a HUGE one – in the price of a coffeemaker I was selling. Instead of around $80, I sold it to someone for $3.99. It hurt like heck to take a loss like that (It cost me around $20 to buy it), but at least I caught it and fixed it before most of my others sold.

13. Read your feedback regularly. I was slammed with three unhappy customers on the same day, which had never happened before. My rating

dropped below 90%, which is awful. I have so far resolved the issues with two of them such that they have removed their negative feedback and my rating has gone back up to 92%.

17

RESOURCES

Books

Retail Arbitrage: The Blueprint for Buying Retail Products to Sell Online for Big Profits – http://amzn.to/chrisgreen Chris Green's book is a must-have. Here is a guy who is passionate about selling online and who is a leading seller on Amazon. His advice on pricing and acquiring inventory is invaluable. He is very analytical and clear about how the numbers, not intuition, drive his buying strategies. Now that you have a basic understanding of Amazon's FBA program and FBAPower, his book will help you go to the next level with your business. He's one of the most down-to-earth people I've ever met and he's genuinely motivated to help people succeed as online sellers.

Selling on Amazon's FBA Program -- by Nathan Holmquist; the book that got me started. He very clearly explains how to sell a penny book for $4 on Amazon with FBA. He is now offering the book free at: http://www.sellfba.com. I paid close to $30 and thought it was well worth it.

The Home-Based Bookstore: Start Your Own Business Selling Used Books on Amazon, eBay or Your Own Web Site – Steve Weber. Steve's written several books including his most recent, *Barcode Booty: How I Found and Sold $2 Million of "Junk" on eBay & Amazon and You Can, Too, Using Your Phone.* When I read *Home-Based*, I felt inspired. He made the business seem very accessible. He focused on book selling but has now expanded since he started using FBAScout. He interviews other sellers in *Booty*, which I found interesting. [Full disclosure: he mentions me as an example in the book on p.22.] Plus, he is a multi-platform seller, which I plan to be down the road. He lists a number of online sites where you can buy inventory at a good price, which I've been checking out over time. www.fatwallet.com has captured my interest lately – there are many other sites to investigate.

Amazon – The Quick and Dirty Guide and *Leftover Gold I & II* – Steve Lindhorst. These books gave me good ideas for sourcing inventory from garage sales to estate sales, warehouse sales, auctions and much more. He gives many examples of finding treasure where other people only saw junk. He also taught me how to make sure my products were worthy of sale on Amazon. He talks about cleaning up books, DVDs and CDs.

Sell Used Books on eBay, Amazon.com and the Internet for Profit – Skip McGrath's book is very helpful for people who want to sell on multiple platforms including eBay, Half.com, Abe Books and others. http://www.skipmcgrath.com/products/sell-used-books-ebay-amazon.php

Creative Sourcing for Booksellers – Frank Aaron Florence. While this book is focused primarily on books, I got several good ideas for places to find cheap inventory. What I've discovered is that there are often cheap DVDs, CDs, software and computer games at the same places where you find books.

The Long Tail: Why the Future of Business is Selling Less of More – Chris Anderson. If this book doesn't convince you there's a buyer for darn near everything, nothing will. It explains why Amazon is successful and why it will continue to be successful. There's an updated version out [http://amzn.to/lessofmore].

Helpful Websites, Groups and Bloggers

FBA Radio – www.fbaradio.com is a new online radio show that airs twice a week. One session is topic oriented (like "Preparing for Black Friday") and one is mentor-oriented where experts answer questions from the chat room. So far it has been dynamite. All episodes are posted online. Chris Green is one of the hosts and they have terrific guests every week. These are seasoned online sellers who have opened my mind to the possibilities. I listen in the evening while listing my books!

FBA Forum -- http://bit.ly/fbaforum is a Yahoo group for FBA sellers. There are over 1400 members and the forum is very active. This is a helpful group where newcomers can get advice from more experienced sellers and seasoned sellers can learn new things to grow their businesses. The archives will hold the answers to many of your questions. It is a closed and monitored/facilitated group. You need to be accepted first. Bob Wiley keeps the group focused on FBA-related issues.

FBAPower – www.fbapower.com. **There is a lot of information on this site including** Scanfob **discounts and videos. There is even a "how-to" video showing how you can scan and read your FBAScout one-handed. Chris is a machine when he is scanning. Go here to sign up for a free one-month trial:** http://bit.ly/2freeweeks. **You'll want to "like" FBAPower's** Facebook (http://www.facebook.com/pages/FBAPower/279593804209 **) page for daily deals and insights.**

Nathan Holmquist – **"Book to the Future" is the name of his blog,** www.booktothefuture.com

Skip McGrath – **a veteran of online sales. He started with eBay and now sells on multiple platforms.** http://www.skipmcgrath.com/newsletters/current.shtml. **He has a blog and books.**

Book Sale Locators

Book Sale Finder – **this free online service is a billboard of many book sales across the country. The sale hosts (usually libraries), list their sales. While it is not comprehensive, it is very helpful. Most of the "mega-sales" of 50,000+ books use Book Sale Finder.** www.booksalefinder.com

Book Sale Manager – this free service includes upcoming sales and offers the additional tool of organizing your book sales, placing them in Outlook or Gmail for you, and sending reminders of the ones you've chosen. It will even download location information to your GPS device. www.booksalemanager.com

Book Sales Found – This is a paid service by Frank Florence that provides a shortcut to finding book sales in your area. What his team does is compile a database of book sales in your area where there isn't a lot of competition, (i.e. not the "cattle calls") and provides you with maps and information. You can even get custom research. You also get his book *Creative Sourcing* (see above) free. I paid $27 for the book and thought it was well worth it. Follow this link and you will get a 7-day free trial and the book. After 7-days, it costs $19.97 a month to continue. http://bit.ly/booksalesfound

Supplies

www.amazon.com – Some of your best deals and many items are FBA (assuming you are a Prime member). Now that Amazon is your website, too, you'll find yourself using it often.

www.uline.com – for inexpensive shipping supplies including boxes, tape, sticker removal solvent.

www.fast-pack.com/bubblewrap.html – Bubble wrap Appreciation Day (an annual national holiday, believe it or not) is the last Monday of January every year and Fast-pack has great sales to celebrate. They have frequent sales and deals throughout the rest of the year as well and sell a lot more than bubble wrap. Their shipping costs are quite reasonable so if you are not near an Uline warehouse, Fast-Pack might be a good solution. Their warehouse is in Lee, Florida.

<u>Online deals</u>

There are many sites, including your favorite retailers, where you can scout for deals. I've tried some purchases from Toys "R" Us and was not impressed - the toys looked beat to death, not cool, inside their boxes. But I've scouted out some items online at other stores that I'm going to try. If you can combine a good deal with free shipping, you get an extra bonus of a free shipping box. Some sites have coupons, point systems, cash-back...you get the idea. I find scouting online much slower than in the store. I'm waiting for Amazon or FBAPower to create a "scout" tool that will work for online sites, I guess. If you live far away from stores, online scouting for deals may be very appealing for you. I've just started my research so this list is not comprehensive:

Big Lots – www.biglots.com. They have regular sales and will notify you in advance if you are a Club member. They also have a wholesale warehouse, if you have a sales tax ID, where the prices are terrific and the bulk purchase requirements are not too onerous ($500 minimum order + 15% shipping cost).

Overstock – www.overstock.com. Just like it sounds, this site sells manufacturers' overstocks. Be careful that you are not buying a refurbished product or a "second" unless the item is for sale on Amazon as a refurbish. You want new-in-box.

Toys "R" Us – www.toysrus.com. and www.babiesrus.com. I'm not impressed with the quality of products in their warehouse but will probably try another time just to see if the three shipments I've had so far were just bad luck. There are online-only sales, coupons and special store deals that you can only find out about online.

Fat Wallet – www.fatwallet.com. This site consolidates deals from all over the internet and keeps a database of "Black Friday" deals as they are leaked. As of this writing in October, they have already posted the Black Friday deals for several retailers.

Woot – www.woot.com. Woot is fun just for its product descriptions. They have super deals but you can't order more than 3 at a time. However if your spouse orders 3, you order 3, your kid orders 3...you can still get quite a few. They have one deal a day and it goes out right after midnight. Once their stock sells out, it's over. Besides regular Woot, they have one for kid products, t-shirts (highly addictive) and wine.

eBay – www.ebay.com. Colleagues of mine have scooped up terrific bargains on eBay to re-sell on Amazon. eBay allows you to set up searches and notifications such that you can be notified if an auction of interest to you is closing. If there aren't other bidders, you can walk away with an amazing bargain. Sometimes an inexperienced seller will make a mistake in the listing that will keep potential buyers away (a misspelling in the title, for example).

Amazon – www.amazon.com. Not to miss the obvious! There are many Amazon sellers who are also inexperienced and who sell products for ridiculously low prices. This is usually because they don't understand their repricer or they don't understand the FBA program. Suddenly a $20 book is selling for 1 penny. Should you buy it? Of course! It will show up at your door in 2 days for only 1 penny to you (assuming you are an Amazon Prime member).

18

Checklist of To-Do's

1. Plan

- ☐ Decide how much money you can spend on supplies and inventory to start.

- ☐ Determine how much you need to make in order for this to be worthwhile.

- ☐ Decide the name of your business.

- ☐ Will you incorporate or just use a DBA to start? (DBA= "Doing Business As")

- ☐ You do not need to decide now if you want to incorporate, but make a note to yourself to think about it later. You may want to read the *Inc. and Grow Rich* book I list in the "Resources" chapter at the end of the book.

2. **Set up your business**

☐ Get your desired DBA from your state. Texas has an online database you can search to find out if the name you want is available. Then you pay a small fee to "own" it for 10 years.

☐ Go online to www.irs.gov and request a business tax ID number in the name of your DBA or corporation. You do not need to be incorporated to get this.

☐ File for your state sales tax number (you can do it online in most states) so you can buy merchandise tax-free.

☐ Open a separate checking account for your business. It does not have to be a business checking account per se, but needs to be separate from your personal account(s) for tax purposes and for ease of accounting.

☐ Sign up for a UPS business account online using your DBA.

☐ Review Amazon's latest fees and set up a spreadsheet of your own to help you determine your break-even point and minimum selling prices.

3. Order supplies

   Depending on your beginning resources, order/source these supplies. The first three are critical to start. See chapters three, eight and the "Resources" at the end of the book for specifics on where to get these items.

   ☐ USB hand-held scanner that plugs into a USB port on your computer.

   ☐ Shipping boxes (18x12x12 or smaller works well for books)

   ☐ Packing tape and paper (or bubble wrap or air pillows – NO foam peanuts)

   ☐ Free UPS shipping labels (two per 8.5" x11" page). You need to sign up and wait about 3-4 days until you can make your first order.

   ☐ Dymo LabelWriter 450 Turbo printer (or a Zebra printer)

   ☐ Address-sized labels for your Dymo printer (from 1"x2" to 2"x3" in size)

   ☐ Smartphone-- FBAScout runs on Android and iPhone phones. Amazon sells cell phones as low as one cent with a two-year contract, so be sure to check that out if you need a phone.

- ☐ Scanfob Bluetooth scanner to use with your smartphone

- ☐ Lanyard for Scanfob

- ☐ Protective carrier for your Smartphone. (I use an armband.)

- ☐ Shipping scale that calculates weights up to at least 75 lbs.

4. Round up your inventory from around the house

- ☐ Books

- ☐ DVDs

- ☐ CDs

- ☐ Video games

- ☐ Software

- ☐ Anything new still sealed in its original packaging

5. Set up your Amazon seller account and FBAPower

- ☐ See chapter 10 for step-by-step instructions

☐ Scan, price and label your items

☐ "Ship" your items from FBAPower to Amazon Seller Central

6. Send in your first shipment

☐ See chapter eleven

☐ Pack and weigh your box(es)

☐ Go through the 7-step shipment process on Seller Central

☐ Take your box(es) to a UPS drop site or arrange a pick-up

7. Go shopping for more inventory

☐ Set up your Scanfob and smartphone. See chapter twelve

☐ Determine the locations of your local Big Lots, Toys "R" Us, Dollar General, TJMaxx, Marshall's, Tuesday Morning (and so on), thrift stores, and library branches. See Chapter Six for ideas of where to find inventory

☐ Find local book sales by calling your library branches or looking at their "Friends" sites online, checking out newspapers and looking at sites like these: www.booksalefinder.com, www.booksalemanager.com

- ☐ Look for garage and estate sales that advertise lots of books

- ☐ Note all local church/temple rummage sales in your calendar as they occur throughout the year – they'll occur about the same time again next year

Cynthia Stine has 23 years of strategic consulting, PR/marketing, business development and communications experience that has included launching dozens of companies and bringing literally hundreds of products to market in such diverse industries as high technology, data communications, Internet, telecommunications, retail, consumer goods, energy, healthcare and financial services. She has worked with both public and private companies and helped several venture-funded companies achieve successful IPOs through strategic communications. She's launched such technologies as the world's first pen-based computer, DSL technology, VOIP and the world's first flywheel battery.

She has owned her own business since 1994 including PRTek, a high-tech public relations agency she sold in 2001; PUBLISH for Success, an independent publisher of non-fiction books sold to a partner in 2006; Promote Success, a full-service PR firm in Dallas; and MyPromote Books, a book consulting and publishing firm which also sells products online through its used book division.

During her career, Cynthia has consistently served as a mentor to other small- business owners. She strongly believes that the future workforce will increasingly consist of self-directed individuals working collaboratively rather than a traditional big-company command-and-control infrastructure.

It is natural, then, that she would be drawn to online sales where a small fish can carve up its piece of a big pond and where working collaboratively ensures greater prosperity for all.

If you would like to talk with Cynthia about your Amazon business, she offers several training and consulting options to help get you started. Learn more at: www.fbastepbystep.com.